JESUS
SPEAKS

JESUS
SPEAKS

LEARNING TO RECOGNIZE &
RESPOND TO THE LORD'S VOICE

LEONARD SWEET AND FRANK VIOLA

W PUBLISHING GROUP

AN IMPRINT OF THOMAS NELSON

Published in Nashville, Tennessee, by W Publishing, an imprint of Thomas Nelson.

Published in association with the literary agency of Daniel Literary Group, Nashville, TN 37027.

Thomas Nelson titles may be purchased in bulk for educational, business, fund-raising, or sales promotional use. For information, please e-mail SpecialMarkets@ThomasNelson.com.

Any Internet addresses, phone numbers, or company or product information printed in this book are offered as a resource and are not intended in any way to be or to imply an endorsement by Thomas Nelson, nor does Thomas Nelson vouch for the existence, content, or services of these sites, phone numbers, companies, or products beyond the life of this book.

Unless otherwise noted, Scripture quotations are taken from the Holy Bible, New International Version®, NIV®. Copyright © 1973, 1978, 1984, 2011 by Biblica, Inc.® Used by permission of Zondervan. All rights reserved worldwide. www.zondervan.com. The "NIV" and "New International Version" are trademarks registered in the United States Patent and Trademark Office by Biblica, Inc.® Scripture quotations marked DARBY are from the Darby Translation. Public domain. Scripture quotations marked ESV are from the ESV® Bible (The Holy Bible, English Standard Version®). Copyright © 2001 by Crossway, a publishing ministry of Good News Publishers. Used by permission. All rights reserved. Scripture quotations marked GNT are from the Good News Translation in Today's English Version—Second Edition. Copyright 1992 by American Bible Society. Used by permission. Scripture quotations marked HCSB are from the Holman Christian Standard Bible®. Copyright © 1999, 2000, 2002, 2003, 2009 by Holman Bible Publishers. Used by permission. HCSB® is a federally registered trademark of Holman Bible Publishers. Scripture quotations marked KJ21 are taken from the 21st Century King James Version®, copyright © 1994. Used by permission of Deuel Enterprises, Inc., Gary, SD 57237. All rights reserved. Scripture quotations marked KJV are from the King James Version. Public domain. Scripture quotations marked THE MESSAGE are from The Message. Copyright © by Eugene H. Peterson 1993, 1994, 1995, 1996, 2000, 2001, 2002. Used by permission of Tyndale House Publishers, Inc. Scripture quotations marked NASB are from New American Standard Bible®. Copyright © 1960, 1962, 1963, 1968, 1971, 1972, 1973, 1975, 1977, 1995 by The Lockman Foundation. Used by permission. (www.Lockman.org). Scripture quotations marked NKJV are from the New King James Version®. © 1982 by Thomas Nelson. Used by permission. All rights reserved. Scripture quotations marked NLT are from the Holy Bible, New Living Translation. © 1996, 2004, 2007, 2013 by Tyndale House Foundation. Used by permission of Tyndale House Publishers, Inc., Carol Stream, Illinois 60188. All rights reserved. Scripture quotations marked NRSV are from New Revised Standard Version Bible. Copyright © 1989 National Council of the Churches of Christ in the United States of America. Used by permission. All rights reserved. Scripture quotations marked PHILLIPS are from The New Testament in Modern English by J. B. Phillips. Copyright © 1960, 1972 J. B. Phillips. Administered by the Archbishops' Council of the Church of England. Used by permission. Scripture quotations marked WUEST are from The New Testament: An Expanded Translation by Kenneth S. Wuest (Grand Rapids: Eerdmans, 1961). Scripture quotations marked YLT are from Young's Literal Translation. Public domain.

Italics in Scripture quotations reflect the authors' added emphasis.

ISBN 978-0-7180-3220-3 (HC)
ISBN 978-0-7180-3828-1 (eBook)

Library of Congress Cataloging-in-Publication Data
Library of Congress Control Number: 2016933597

Printed in the United States of America
16 17 18 19 20   RRD   10 9 8 7 6 5 4 3 2 1

CONTENTS

Contents

Contents

"My sheep hear My voice, and I know them, and they follow Me."

—JOHN 10:27 NASB

How to Read This Book

This book is a combination of storytelling and practical instruction. Within these pages, we'll be taking you on an exciting journey with the risen Christ found in Scripture while giving you practical handles on how to hear His voice today.

Our aim is threefold. First, we want to give you a firm foundation in the Scriptures concerning how Jesus spoke to His disciples. We want to introduce you to the scriptures that highlight Jesus' resurrection voice. Each encounter that Jesus had with His disciples in His postresurrection appearances is told in a story with multiple layers of meaning. We will unpack those for you.

Second, we want to dispel the myths and misinformation surrounding what it means to hear the voice of Jesus today. If you're like we are, when someone says, "The Lord told me . . . ," it can be a bit unsettling, even mystifying. But the truth is that Jesus speaks to all of His followers today—even you. And He speaks in many different ways. We want to demystify those ways for you. We also want to explain how you can cultivate a rich experience and a growing relationship with Jesus simply by hearing His voice.

Lastly, we tell stories because Jesus told stories—stories filled with narratives and metaphors (Len calls them "narraphors") that speak directly to the heart. The stories surrounding the resurrected Christ, the people He encountered, and what He said and did for them before ascending to heaven are informative, purposeful, lyrical, and sacred. The way Jesus continues to speak today from heaven is no less inspired.

Two Volumes Under One Cover

With those goals in mind, we've divided *Jesus Speaks* into two volumes.

In volume 1, written by Leonard, we'll hear the stories of how Jesus Christ spoke to His followers after His resurrection. Because Jesus is the same yesterday, today, and forever (Heb. 13:8), the various ways He spoke in the New Testament are the same ways in which He speaks today. This section is full of transforming insights and reflections based on the gospel material and the book of Acts.

In volume 2, written by Frank, we bring the discussion closer to home with a nuts-and-bolts analysis of *how* to hear Jesus today. With so many people claiming to hear the voice of God, and countless others who feel frustrated in trying to hear Him, we believe a clear, scripturally based application that dispels the fog on this issue is in order. So volume 2 is highly practical. And our instruction goes way beyond the not-so-helpful canned answer, "Just pray and read your Bible."

In short, volume 1 gives you the big picture of how the resurrected Jesus spoke in the New Testament and why this knowledge is critical today. The chapters are robust, poetic in style, and filled with metaphorical language.

Volume 2 gets down to brass tacks. The chapters are deliberately short, actionable, and filled with scriptural quotes and references, so that readers can see that we're rooting our conclusions in timeless truth rather than imagination or armchair philosophy, as some authors have done in the past.

While both volumes are different in content and style, they are complementary, working together to elucidate how to recognize and respond to the voice of Jesus today in our own lives.

Three Reading Plans

Given the way we formatted the chapters, there are three different ways—or plans—in which you can read this book.

Plan 1: Read it like any traditional book, from beginning to end. So you'd read volume 1 and then volume 2.

Plan 2: Reverse the order. There's no harm in starting with volume 2, especially if you want to begin with the shorter, practical chapters. You can then read volume 1 afterward.

Plan 3: At the end of each chapter in volume 1, you'll find a reference to the corresponding practical chapters in volume 2. So you can switch between reading volume 1 and volume 2 by following the references at the end of each chapter in volume 1.

Regardless of what plan you use, our hope is that by reading this little book, you will be better equipped to hear the voice of the Lord for yourself. And thereby, your relationship with Jesus will deepen, your service will be informed, and your life will be enriched.

Let's begin the journey . . .

—Leonard Sweet and Frank Viola

The Whispers of God's Voice

"Blessed are the eyes that see what you see! For I tell you that many prophets and kings desired to see what you see, and did not see it, and to hear what you hear, and did not hear it."

LUKE 10:23–24 ESV

A youth group leader took his kids to a ski resort, where he saw two people skiing down the slopes one behind the other. They were so close it was almost as if they were tied together. When he got closer, he heard the one in front saying in staccato fashion, "Left." "Right." "Straight." "Right." "Left."

He thought it was a little funny, and his kids were laughing at the sound of what looked like a ski instructor giving lessons to a student. So he thought he'd have a little fun with the student skier. He started yelling out different commands that contradicted the ski instructor. When the person in front said, "Left," he'd yell, "Right!" When the person in front said, "Straight," he'd yell, "Curve!" But no matter what the youth leader said, the student in back seemed to be able to ignore his voice and fix on what the ski instructor was saying.

Suddenly the skier stopped and turned around. Much to the

embarrassment of the youth leader, on the chest of the second skier was a sign: Blind Skier.

Even though he could see nothing, since he knew his instructor's voice, the blind skier could ignore all other voices—even those tempting and tormenting him—and go safely down the slopes.

The Voice

A large segment of Christians claim that God speaks to them. One of us grew up in a movement where the phrase *The Lord told me* was the order of the day. "The Lord told me to call my friend." "The Lord showed me whom to marry." "This morning I was in my kitchen and the Lord said to call my mother." And similar reports.

The result is that an even larger segment of the Christian community is left feeling, "Why doesn't the Lord speak to me like that?" Or worse, "What's wrong with me? Why can't I hear the Lord like these other people do?" The result: We have people claiming that the Lord speaks to them constantly. And we have others who feel God is giving them the cold shoulder.

Either way, countless Christians today desperately want to know how to hear the voice of their Savior. But if they are honest, they will admit they don't quite know how. If this describes you, then this book was written for you.

In this volume, we aim to make one simple yet critical assertion: Jesus Christ is always speaking to His followers. It is up to us to learn how to recognize His voice. And when we do learn to identify His voice, it becomes as familiar as our own heartbeats.

If you are one of the Lord's true sheep, your heart is already attuned to hear His voice. Now you just need to learn how to distinguish it from all of the other voices jamming your frequencies. Radio stations are constantly sending their unique signals through the airwaves. But unless a person's radio is tuned to a particular frequency, he will never pick up the signals.

Hearing the voice of Jesus Christ is much the same. Because Jesus dwells within every genuine believer through the Holy Spirit, He is always speaking, always leading, always revealing. And He speaks in many different ways.

Sometimes Jesus speaks in a whisper.

Sometimes Jesus speaks in a still, small voice, easy on the ear.

Sometimes Jesus thunders and shouts, beating hard on the eardrum.

Sometimes all you hear is the sound of silence.

But Jesus is always speaking.

Job talks about the whispers of God's voice like this: "And these are but the outer fringe of his works; how faint the whisper we hear of him! Who then can understand the thunder of his power?" (Job 26:14).

At times in life you may be a sitting Job, crushed with grief and pain, struggling to believe in a God you can't hear anymore.

At times in life you may be a jumping Jehoshaphat, barely able to contain the "Hallelujahs!" of your soul.

At times in life you may be a weeping Jeremiah, bent over and wanting to quit, because you have heard a message you didn't want to deliver to a people you are sick and tired of serving after a lifetime of talking to a brick wall.

The registers of Jesus speaking record the seasons of your soul.

The Ear

The psalmist asked, "He who planted the ear, does he not hear?" (Ps. 94:9 ESV). The primary gateway to the soul is the ear. By definition, the disciples of faith are first and foremost listeners. The very word *disciple* means "the one who listens and learns." The very word *faith* is based on hearing, not seeing: "Faith comes from what is heard" (Rom. 10:17 HCSB), "the evidence of things not seen" (Heb. 11:1 KJV). Our ears need opening if we are to hear Jesus speak.

In India, there are street ear cleaners. Standing in line at the theater, you might be approached by such a peddler promising to give your ears a good cleaning. Imagine if everyone could get their ears cleaned before worship. What if everyone had someone to let them know when their ears were blocked to the voice of Jesus and needed a good cleaning out?

What if there were a place you could go in which your ears could be especially attuned, ready to receive the voice of God?

The word that gives its name to "cathedral," *cathedra*, refers to a seat or chair, specifically the chair of a bishop, a seat of learning and listening. In some traditions, the *cathedra* is a holy place of learning and listening. In those traditions, to speak *ex cathedra* is to speak with the full authority of the chair on which one is sitting. Something spoken *ex cathedra* means the whole weight of one's office is behind what one is saying.

Every follower of Jesus needs a chair, a "seat," of learning and listening. Have you cleared a space in your life where you can put the chair? A spot where you can stop, sit, and listen? It is hard to hear Jesus when we are living such busy lives and our hearts are filled with noise, not silence or stillness.

And it is hard to hear Jesus when we are always talking.

Inuit artists from the top of the Arctic Circle, a place known as Repulse Bay, are famous for their ivory carvings. One of the most collected Inuit artists, Mark Tungilik (1913–1986), was once asked why the figures in his carvings had gaping mouths. Tungilik said that they represented white men, who are "always talking." You can't hear God if you are listening to yourself.

The first mission of love is to listen.

If you listen, you will hear.

Two Kinds of Hearing

Scripture presents a paradox when it comes to hearing the voice of Jesus. In John chapter 10, the Lord plainly said, "My sheep hear my voice" (v. 27 KJV). So the Good Shepherd speaks to His sheep, and His sheep unfailingly hear His voice. But Jesus also said this to His beloved sheep, "Whoever has ears, let them hear" (Rev. 2:7). Here Jesus says that the one who "has ears" must "hear" His voice. If Jesus asks us to hear, then it is not automatic.

How do we resolve this conflict?

It's the difference between having a sound wave hit your eardrum (hearing) and discerning what's being said and who is saying it (recognition).

Imagine you're talking to a friend who is reading an e-mail on her smartphone. As you are talking, she interrupts you saying, "Can you repeat what you just said? I wasn't listening." Your friend heard that you were saying something, but didn't really hear what you said. So she didn't discern what you said because her attention was focused elsewhere.

Every minute, we are bombarded with signals from television and radio moving through the air we breathe. But unless we have a tuner that picks up those signals, we won't recognize them. Along these lines, the fundamental action word in the Bible as it concerns the voice of the living God is not *obey* or *submit*.

It is *listen*.

So while the Lord frequently speaks to us and we "hear" His voice, we don't really hear it unless we recognize it. This book is an exploration of what it means to listen with both sets of ears. Our goal is to teach you how to recognize the voice that's always speaking.

"Whoever has ears, let them hear what the Spirit says to the churches."
—REVELATION 2:11

Hearing the Voice of the Resurrected Jesus in the Stories of Scripture

ONE

The Unexpected Voice of Jesus

Jesus' First Appearance: Jesus Speaks to Mary in the Garden

It was daybreak and the sun arose,
Together with him some stars,
When the Divine Love
First moved its beautiful works.

DANTE, INFERNO[1]

What gave rise to Christianity? The belief that Jesus rose from the dead. Can you hear Him rising in you every day? The risen Christ gives rise to a life of surprise and enterprise. Rise up! Hear the unexpected voice of the risen Christ!

The first rise up was at sunrise. In all of the Gospels, the first resurrection experiences happen "early and dark." God's favorite time to walk and talk with us is early and dark or in the fade of light. The old saying "The early bird catches the worm" is actually a loose translation of the old German saying *"Morgenstunde hat Gold im Mund,"* or "The morning hours have gold in their mouth."[2] In the morning hours, God magically spins the garbage of our lives into pure gold.

The gold-mine times of day are dawn and dusk. Ask any gardener, and he will tell you that the best time to walk a garden is when "the dew drops from heaven"—early and dark, late and light. Dawn and dusk are when God walked and talked in the garden with the First Adam. Dawn and dusk are when the Last Adam walked and talked with His Father. Early and dark was Jesus' favorite time of day.[3] Maybe prayer is nothing more nor less than walking and talking with God. Maybe prayer is simply a conversation with God about "How does your garden grow?" Maybe prayer is simply a panning for gold, as God strains our lives of dust and dirt. Maybe prayer is simply a song sung at dawn (aubade) or dusk (serenade) by your lover under your bedroom window.

The Daybreak Voice

God's voice may often be heard most clearly at daybreak, in the in-between hour when it's darkest and creation is dawning. But you have to be awake—awake to life, aware of Jesus' presence, alert to His voice—to hear Jesus speak in His daybreak voice. God's "loving heart," God's heart of gold, "visits us like the dawn from on high" (Luke 1:78, author's paraphrase). The dawn reveals secrets that the day conceals. When the day dawns, does the morning star rise in your heart?

Matthew 28, Mark 16, Luke 24, and John 20 each open with the arrival of the women (including Mary Magdalene) at the tomb.

They found it empty with the stone rolled away. Mary Magdalene separated from the other women to find Peter and John, while the rest of them went to find the other nine disciples to inform them of the empty tomb.

Peter and John ran to the tomb, and after they found the body missing, the limestone slab bookended by a stack of grave clothes and the folded shroud, they ran back to join the other nine. Mary Magdalene remained behind and through the prism of her tears saw two angels. Mary *heard* the angels' voices, where John and Peter had only *seen* dirty laundry.

The Angelic Voice

Sometimes you hear Jesus smuggle His voice into your life through an encounter with an angel. Whenever an angel shows up in the Bible, something life-changing and earth-shaking is about to happen. Life gets complicated. Angels must know we know this—that the fact you see them means, "This is going to scare the pants off of you, but . . ." So that's why the first words out of an angel's mouth are often "Fear not," or in today's lingo, "It's okay! Don't be afraid!"

Just as Mary, mother of Jesus, believed the impossible when an angel appeared to her and she embraced the new life inside her, so now Mary Magdalene, Jesus' friend and follower, believed the impossible when two angels appeared to her, and she embraced the new life in front of her.

Your baptism makes you a candidate for consorting with an angel. Some angels wear wings; some, cuffs. Some angels appear as humans.[4]

When you are baptized, there grows a new life inside you, summoning you to fearlessly embrace the impossible. Of course, you can starve the miracle inside you. That way you'll never be bothered by angels.

There is an old story about when God created human beings. The angels were jealous because God had endowed the humans with divine wisdom that would guide them through life. So the jealous angels conspired to hide a certain gift from the humans.

"Let's take it to the peak of the highest mountain," said one.

"No," said another. "Let's bury it at the bottom of the deepest sea."

But the smartest angel of all said, "Let's hide divine wisdom deep inside each person. It's the last place they'll ever look."

The positive human traits of creativity, imagination, compassion, altruism, conscience, intuition, the "better angels of our nature," often stem from interior voices, not exterior ones. Or in the words of John Wesley, "Sometimes a strong impression, for which we are not able to give any account, is not altogether to be despised."[5]

After her angelic visitation, Mary stumbled out of the tomb, into the light, and almost literally bumped into Jesus. She assumed He was the

Do not neglect to show hospitality to strangers, for thereby some have entertained angels unawares.

—HEBREWS 13:2 ESV

gardener, a biblical "sign" that Jesus' mission was complete and the Last Adam had restored us to the garden relationship with God for which we were made.

Some bumps in the night belong to both sleeping and waking worlds. Some bumps in the road are actually Jesus interrupting our journey to remind us that the journey is not everything. Those destination moments—and admittedly they're rare—when "the fish grabs the fly," when the divine intersects the human, are why you endure and enjoy the journey to begin with. When these destination moments happen with Jesus, as Mary discovered here, and as the disciples discovered a short time later, what a divine kettle of fish!

The Naming Voice

What's in a name? Ask Mary.

God wants to speak to us *by name.* Just as in Genesis 3 when God hunted Adam and Eve down and asked, "Adam, Eve, where are you?" Jesus initiated the encounter with Mary by speaking her name.

Once she heard her name, she knew He was not the gardener, but the Master Gardener, her Lord and Messiah. Once Jesus speaks your name, you know who He is, and who you are. But first we have to hear Him speak.

Jesus told Mary to tell others that He is alive, and she became the first evangelist, the "apostle to the apostles." As Mark 16:9–11 explains, Mary Magdalene was the first to whom the Lord appeared, but the disciples did not believe her story.

After appearing to Mary Magdalene, Jesus visited the women who were running to the city, and He reinforced the message that they should go tell His brethren that they would see Him in Galilee.

Perhaps Jesus made this personal appearance to these women because they were so terribly afraid and too fearful to speak to anyone (Mark 16:8). After He met them, they joyfully delivered the message. Luke 24:9–11 summarizes the fact that "the eleven and . . . all the rest" (NKJV) ultimately heard about Christ's resurrection from the women, including Mary Magdalene. Yet no one believed them.

Every baptism is an individual cutting of the covenant into the physical body of those "who believe in His name" (John 1:12 NKJV). We are not called to lose our identity in some mystical Borg body, but to find our identity by losing ourselves in Christ and laying down our lives for the sake of others. Pope John Paul II hated the word *crowd* because of its implications of anonymity. He preferred the word *multitudes*. "Each person is unique," he said, "and I was anxious to preserve the personal contact of each relationship."[6] Jesus names names. We are not just people in a crowd for Jesus. Jesus knows us by name.

In fact, each one of our names is engraved "on the palms of [God's] hands" (Isa. 49:16). Or since that phrase is better translated "I have carved your name on the face of my cliff,"[7] then that means God cannot forget us any more than a nursing mother can forget her suckling child (v. 15) or any more than the citizens of Egypt can forget who is king. Ancient kings carved their names on the cliffs on the borders of their kingdoms to remind anyone entering or leaving the kingdom of who was really in charge. Six thousand years later, we can still see these cartouches carved on the cliff walls in the deserts of Egypt. God honors us by recording our names in a format that cannot ever be erased, even after thousands of years.

And we can never be the same again.

The Transfiguring Voice

When Mary recognized Jesus and tried to ground Him to earth with her grasp (John 20:16–17), Jesus instructed Mary to let go and go tell His disciples what she had seen, that He is risen and among them once again. Mary, the apostle to the apostles, ran to report this amazing, miraculous news.

"Do not cling to Me," Jesus told Mary (v. 17 NKJV). God does not always meet our expectations. Mary didn't want to let Jesus out of her sight again. Mary didn't want to let Him go. Mary didn't want things to change. But everything had changed.

Everything *has* changed. We listen to Christ not simply to comprehend Him or to communicate with Him but to be changed into His image. The goal of listening to Jesus is not so we can impersonate Him, but so we can personate Him. To hear and heed the risen Lord is to be changed. A theology of change is at the heart of Christianity. But what kind of change is this change? Is it *metanoia* or metamorphosis? Is it transformation or transfiguration?

If you could reduce the gospel to one word, most scholars would choose *metanoia*—the Greek word translated "repentance" in the New Testament.[8] *Metanoia* represents the message of John the Baptist, who proclaimed a "baptism of repentance [*metanoia*]" in Mark 1:4. *Metanoia* represents the first preaching of Jesus, when He called on people to "repent [*metanoeo*], for the kingdom of heaven has come near" (Matt. 4:17). *Metanoia* represents the message of Jesus' disciples when they "preached that people should repent [*metanoeo*]" (Mark 6:12). *Metanoia* represents St. Paul's assertion in Acts 17:30 that God commands "all people everywhere to repent [*metanoeo*]." Jesus even used the noun form of the word once: "I have not come to call the righteous, but sinners to repentance [*metanoia*]" (Luke 5:32).

Most of the time we translate both "*meta-noeo*" and "*meta-noia*," or literally "change of [*meta*] mind [*noia*]," as "repentance." Some have called the translation of *metanoia* as "repentance" the "worst mistranslation in the New Testament." Some have translated it as a "turnaround," a 180-degree change of direction.[9] That is almost as bad, as if Jesus only takes us on a detour.

The Aramaic of *metanoia* really means a "returning home." When

Jesus restores the original image of God in us, when we become new creatures in Christ, when "old things have passed away; behold, all things have become new" (2 Cor. 5:17 NKJV), we are learning how to be the original humans God made us to be. We are returning home. "So if anyone is in Christ, there is a new creation," Paul said to the church at Corinth (v. 17 NRSV). To be "in Christ" is to do life in new and exciting ways.

John the Baptist said, "I baptize you with *metanoia*; the One who comes will baptize you with fire."[10] A baptism of *metanoia* is not simply a mere turning to God or a life change. A baptism of *metanoia* is a true metamorphosis, a returning home to the original life God created us for. We are talking about a total metamorphosis—a total change of mind, heart, and body. Before Jesus spoke Mary's name, the dominant language used was *metanoia*. After Jesus spoke Mary's name, the dominant language used was metamorphosis. *Metanoia* is more than transformation, which is outside-in change. *Metanoia* is transfiguration, which is inside-out change.

The question of the rich young ruler showcases the nature of the difference: "What must I *do* to inherit eternal life?" (Luke 18:18). Our immediate default is to believe and trust in the virtues of doing something over being something. Let's take Micah 6:8 as an example: "He has shown you, O mortal, what is good. And what does the LORD require of you? To *act justly* and to *love mercy* and to *walk humbly* with your God." Jesus did not become one of us to tell us how to *do* humility but to *be* humble; not how to *do* mercy but to *be* merciful; not how to *do* justice but to *be* just. To live in Christ is to live the life of the One in whom justice was fulfilled, mercy perfected, and humility consummated.

Jesus doesn't need our service, our programs, our gifts. Jesus desires our selves, our hearts, our lives. Here is Jesus' rendition of Micah 6:8:

> "Blessed are the meek,
>
>> For they shall inherit the earth. . . .
>
> "Blessed are the merciful
>
>> For they shall obtain mercy. . . .

"Blessed are those who hunger and thirst for righteousness,

For they shall be filled." (Matt. 5:5, 7, 6 NKJV)

When Jesus speaks, we are not merely transformed to do humility, to do mercy, to do justice. We are transfigured into the humble, the merciful, the just human beings God made us to be. To hear Jesus' call to be a disciple is more than doing what Jesus did or preserving "the living memory of Jesus." To be a disciple is to be an internal bearer of the risen Christ. If the ultimate in praying is letting Jesus pray in us, the ultimate in listening is letting Jesus live in us.

Jesus' voice does not put our heads in the sand or in the clouds. The voice of Jesus sets our feet on lofty places and lifts our hands to reach and touch the stars.

The Derailing Voice

Matthew 28:11–15 tells us of another important event on that Sunday morning. The guards told the chief priests what had happened. With the help of bribes in the right places, the chief priests hatched and spread the tale that the disciples had stolen the body while the guards slept. In other words, the guards were willing to incriminate themselves with falsehoods because they lacked the guts to tell the truth. In their deceit, the guards confirmed for all of history that the tomb was really empty.

> *"Whoever has ears to hear, let them hear."*
>
> —JESUS (MARK 4:9)

You will need to sort out Jesus' voice from conflicting, contradicting voices. There will always be voices that claim to be Jesus' voice but are really voices that lead us astray and amok, out of earshot of the divine. Some of these are voices of temptation. Some of these are voices of the self. Some of these are voices of pop culture. We live in a culture obsessed with listening to its own voice, unused to listening for God's voice. Some of these voices are the powers and principalities of the world—deceitful, dishonest voices that create such a din of confusion and disinformation that it is hard to hear the truth amid the dissembling. People are eager to pollute the Well of Living Water with all sorts of contaminants and colorings that dilute and substitute the Word of God.

Most of the time, our hearing problem isn't that Jesus is not speaking; it's our inability to hear Jesus speaking because we're listening to voices other than Jesus' voice. Our antennae have been diverted into the realms of lies and untruths. We have "ears to hear" only the politically correct or the party lines of various establishments. Those with true "ears to hear" choose how to hear, rather than be drawn to reflex responses based on one's social condition, political correctitude, and psychological preprogramming. "Ears-to-hear" responsiveness requires the courage of "response-ability"—which the guards at the tomb lacked.

For the practical application of the themes mentioned in this chapter, see chapters 9–15 in volume 2.

The Hidden Voice of Jesus

Jesus' Second Appearance: Jesus Speaks to
Two Disciples on the Emmaus Road

Before Jesus appeared to the Eleven as a group, He made two recorded appearances to individuals. One was to Mary Magdalene. The other was to Cleopas and his companion on the road to Emmaus. After the couple discovered that their Bible teacher was Jesus, they retraced their steps—to report to the Eleven. Then they discovered that Jesus had a personal meeting with Simon Peter. That meeting with Peter is reported in Luke 24:34, but we have no other details about it.

Jesus' Voice Hidden by Doubt, Agenda, and Grief

There is almost as much uncertainty about where Emmaus was as there is about who these Emmaus disciples were. The earliest texts give the distance as 60 stadia (7 miles), but enough give the distance as 160 stadia (18 miles) to make Amwas a real contender for the location of the city the Bible calls Emmaus. We know that Emmaus was close enough to Jerusalem that one could walk there and back in one day. But that could apply to either distances of 60 or 160 stadia. If the road to Emmaus was the road to Amwas, Jesus could have almost told the whole story of Israel just by pointing out the geographical sites they passed by on their wilderness walk to Emmaus.

Perhaps the very elusiveness of Emmaus suggests something deeper: your Emmaus can be any time and every place. Any moment can be an Emmaus moment. And we all need "Emmaus moments," because faith is activated by events and experiences, not by theories and theologies. Besides, what happens when Jesus speaks is more important than where Jesus speaks.

Who are these two people called the Emmaus disciples? We know one of them was named Cleopas (Luke 24:18). In most of the Renaissance art portraying this scene, these disciples are always two males. Isn't that interesting? No one ever thought they could be a male and a female. And yet when they got to Emmaus, these two disciples invited Jesus to stay in their home. In ancient Middle Eastern terms, this would actually suggest that these two were married.

Cleopas appears somewhere else in the Bible: at the cross. Three Marys stayed beside Jesus through His final hours: His mother Mary; Mary Magdalene; and "his mother's sister, Mary the wife of Clopas" (John 19:25).

We agree with those scholars who believe that Clopas is the same person as Cleopas, which means that these two disciples were husband and wife—Cleopas and Mary.[1]

In addition, it's possible that Mary, Cleopas's wife, was the sister of Jesus' mother (or even father). If this is the case, it means that Cleopas and Mary were the aunt and uncle of Jesus.[2]

Missed Moment

In every single story of Jesus' postresurrection sightings, people didn't recognize Him at first. Each time, the disciples were devastatingly close to missing the most important moment in their lives, the most important moment in the history of the world in fact, because they didn't recognize Jesus. And here, even His relatives failed to see Him for who He is.

Even though they were family, and among the close followers of Jesus, all they now saw and felt was sorrow, disillusion, and bewilderment. They were so beside themselves that they couldn't recognize Jesus, even when He walked and talked beside them. Their faith had been shattered like a pot dropped to the ground. Their hopes had been decimated. They believed in a political Messiah who would deliver them from Roman rule, not a sacrificial Messiah who would release them from their sins and restore them to a right relationship with God. Their belief in everything they thought Jesus was and would be had disintegrated along with their faith in the future He had promised, in the future God had promised.

Jesus' Road Voice

Doubt shatters dreams and blocks our hearing. It may be the most laming illness of the soul. Doubt cannot hear hope or see life. Doubt blocks everything but doubt. Doubt surely can't hear or see the living Jesus beside you. For Cleopas and Mary, doubt and despair had seized their hearts so much that they had decided to return home. They weren't going to remain in Jerusalem with the rest of Jesus' disciples. They had given up. Their hopes were dashed, and, sad and dejected, they despaired of the future.

But the story wasn't over. Jesus comes to us, even in our deepest doldrums, and walks beside us. Can you remember a time in your life when you felt like Uncle Cleopas and Aunt Mary? When the sky was falling, and death seemed so much more powerful than life? When the evil forces of the world seemed to be beating back the good? When you felt alone, hopeless, burdened down with the harsh realities of life? In those times, perhaps you, too, could not recognize Jesus walking beside you. Perhaps in your own brokenness, doubt began to creep in, muffling your eardrums as well as mugging your dreams.

And yet, we know from the Emmaus road story that Jesus journeys with us even when we abandon hope and run away. In fact, it is in our woundedness that Jesus walks and talks with us the most. Jesus reminds us, Jesus prods us, Jesus nudges us to remember "the rock [from] whence [we were] hewn,"[3] the ultimate reality that we block out in our doubt and despair.

Did you notice who initiated the Emmaus road conversation? Jesus did. In fact, how do we even know Cleopas and Mary were vexed and perplexed? Jesus asked them why their chins were down.

Jesus Converses with the Disciples

Jesus was a master questioner. The Gospels are a case study in how to ask great questions—in the Emmaus story, the question was, "Why are you depressed?" In his delightful book *Jesus Asked*, Conrad Gempf argues that if Jesus were to meet you on the street today, He would more likely ask you something than tell you anything.[4] Jesus speaks in questions, which means that questions are our friends, not our enemies. A questioning spirit is a Jesus spirit, and we hear Jesus better the more open we are to experience. David Dark calls it "the sacredness of questioning everything."[5] Be curious, imaginative, and creative if you want to turn up the volume on Jesus' voice. Be conforming, unimaginative, predictable, and uncomfortable with change if you want to mute Jesus' voice.

Jesus created a culture of conversation and questioning wherever He went. It's all about conversation for Jesus. Most of the time, we translate the Greek word *laleó* as "spoke," but it actually means "had a conversation with." So Jesus was walking with Uncle Cleopas and Aunt Mary, conversing with them, when they asked Him, "Are you the only one visiting Jerusalem who does not know the things that have happened there in these days?" (Luke 24:18). In other words, "What rock have you been hiding under?"

And we love Jesus' playful response. The most important event in the history of humanity has occurred the past weekend—and Jesus asked, "What things?" (v. 19).

Jesus Plays and Pretends

First lesson here: Jesus did not reveal His identity immediately but took time with the Emmaus disciples. Slowly He connected dots in the Scriptures as He gently led them deeper and deeper into the story. He showed how the Scriptures had already told the story, and slowly but surely their heads began to get it, and their hearts began to burn. Revelation is a slow burn that accompanies deeper and deeper immersion in the story. In a traditional Roman Catholic rite, the bishop presents a candidate for ordination as a deacon with the "Book of the Gospels," along with some challenging words on how he is to spend his life "hearing the Word." The bishop charges him:

> Receive the Gospel of Christ, whose herald you now are.
>
> Believe what you read,
>
> Teach what you believe
>
> And practice what you teach.

Second lesson here: if worship becomes a work zone, a construction site of plans and graphs, we have missed something. Worship is a playground of the Spirit. So here in Luke 24 we have Jesus playing with His disciples, and they walked and talked together as God did in the garden with Adam and Eve. As they were walking, He explained the story to them. He started at Genesis and went all the way to the maps. He shared about how the whole story fits together.

When they finally got to Emmaus, Cleopas and Mary were so hungry, hungry for food and hungry for more of the story, that they asked the mystery man to stay and join them for a meal. Consistent with

"Do not say [that you don't know how to speak and] that you are too young, but go to the people I send you to. . . . Do not be afraid of them, for I will be with you to protect you."

—JEREMIAH 1:7–8 GNT

Eastern practices of hospitality, Jesus probably declined the first time, since the text says "they urged him strongly" to stay with them (v. 29).

Let's put this in context. When you say to people on the street, "Hey, how are you doing?" you don't really want them to give you a dissertation on their day. They may say, "I'm fine." That's it. It's a social norm. But if you follow it up with, "No, I really mean it. How are you doing?" then you just got serious.

In ancient Eastern hospitality, one might say, "Please stay with us for dinner." It's another cultural norm. You were bound to offer hospitality to the stranger whether you could afford it or not, even if you had nothing in the kitchen and no room in the house. But in the same way, if you refuse and then a person repeats the request—"No, we really mean it. Please stay with us. We don't want this to end"—then they are being serious. This is what transpired in this situation in Emmaus. In pretending to go forward, Jesus was following the conventions of ancient hospitality. And in a repeated insistence that He accept their invitation, Cleopas and Mary indicated the seriousness of their intent.

It was during dinner that something really incredible happened: "When he was at the table with them, he took bread, gave thanks, broke it and began to give it to them" (Luke 24:30).

Jesus' Voice Blows Us Away

If you are in a Jesus story, and you are not being startled, shocked, or scandalized, you are not in the right story. It's the same with Jesus speaking. If you believe you're hearing Jesus speak, and He's saying something bland, boring, or predictable, then it's probably not Jesus you're hearing.

And right here, anyone in the first century would be shocked, scandalized, and startled. Tradition dictated that Cleopas was the head of the table, the one who broke the bread. It was the symbol of his hospitality. It would be the height of Jewish emasculation to allow someone else to break the bread and take the seat of hospitality at your table.

But one of the Emmaus surprises was that Cleopas and Mary became guests in their own home. The roles were reversed, and Jesus broke the bread and handed it to them. Then something even more amazing happened: "Then their eyes were opened and they recognized him" (v. 31).

So the question is, what caused this recognition?

"Then . . . they recognized him." Why "then"?

His aunt and uncle didn't recognize Jesus when they first saw Him. They didn't recognize Him the entire trip to Emmaus as they were walking for seven (or eighteen) miles. They didn't recognize Him when He came into the house. They didn't recognize Him when He sat down at the table.

So what happened when Jesus took the head of the table? He took the bread, blessed it, broke it, and gave it to them . . . *then* they recognized Him! Why *then*?

Why "Then"?

The key to communication in some technological cultures is to turn stories into movies with a soundtrack—to *see* what we are reading in cinematic form, a motion picture in our minds.

It's time to use our imaginations. Picture it in your mind: Jesus assumes the role of host. He takes the bread in His hands, gives the blessing, and breaks the bread. At the moment when He reaches out His hands to pass them the bread, and they reach out to take it, they see . . . what?

His wounds. Because His hands and wrists were exposed.

Then they recognize Him.

We are all Emmaus road disciples. It is in the "breaking of bread" that we recognize Him.

Celebrated as one of the greatest writers of all time, French writer Marcel Proust (1871–1922) filled out a personal questionnaire at the start of his career for a magazine like the one we know today as *Vanity Fair*. His handwritten response sold at auction in 2003 for almost a quarter of a million dollars. One of the questions asked of him was this: "What profession would you have chosen had lack of paper prevented you from becoming a writer?" Proust replied, "I would, I think, have chosen to be a baker: it is honorable to give men their daily bread."[6] Proust realized what every writer, and every disciple, learns, often the hard way: we are fed as we feed. But it is the "breaking" as much as the "eating" of the bread that enables us to see Jesus' wounds.

When Cleopas and Mary saw the wounds, *then* they recognized Him. Their ears and eyes were opened, and they recognized the living, present Jesus there at their table. Their doubt was healed, their despair was dispelled, and their ability to see the truth was empowered. Their faith had kicked in.

Jesus' identity is revealed in wounds and in food. Jesus speaks the loudest in hurts and hungers, tears and tables.

Let's be precise. They didn't see scars. Scars are healed wounds. They saw wounds. Jesus took the wounds of the world with Him into eternity. When Jesus was pierced by the sword as He hung upon the cross, He spilled blood and water, a sign that He actually died on the cross, not from crucifixion but from a broken heart.[7]

Jesus bears that broken heart even now. As long as there is one person not seated at the table, Jesus bears the wounds of humanity even at the right hand of the Father. Jesus' pierced hands, feet, head, back, side, and heart are not scars; they are open wounds.

When the Emmaus disciples saw these wounds, *then* they recognized Him.

They didn't miss their moment. Will you?

Our Moment of Recognition

It is our mission to hear Jesus speak even if not in words. It is our moment to miss, or our moment to discover. It is the most important moment in your life, and still the most important moment in the history of humanity. Are you missing your moment? Are you missing Jesus in the world?

Do you want to hear Jesus speak? Go to where the wounds are. Find wounded people, hurting people, suffering people, and you will find Jesus.

Where are the people in your community who are weary, bleeding, maimed by life, and oppressed by injustice? Where are people being bullied and attacked? Where are there wounds still fresh?

Do you have a "bleeding heart" for people?

Do you have "wounded" hands and feet from getting down and dirty, walking with the wounded in their valleys and rocky places?

Do you live within earshot of the cries of the hurting and hungry?

Do you bind up hearts that are broken (Isa. 61:1–3)?

If you want to hear Jesus, go to the wounded. The church is where wounds become scars through the blood of Jesus, and where those who carry scars know what it means to be sincere bearers of the cross.[8]

Hidden Wounds and Revealed Wounds

We live in a wounded world, a pierced planet. We are all wounded people. The church, the body of Christ, ought to be the place where the wounded gather.

The church is the wounded body of Jesus in and for a wounded world. The church is made up of wounded people who are being made whole and beautiful by the glue of grace, which comes from the blood of Christ. The church is a wounded body that rises above its brokenness and becomes a visage of Christ.

Brokenness is critical for hearing the Lord.

First, brokenness brings openness to hearing. The breaking of bread is God's breaking the spell of fear and opening us to daily dependence on Him. When we stockpile our resources for rainy days and remove our neediness, we are removing our need for God. This may be the hardest part of hearing Jesus for those who hate being needy. For proud givers and nervous receivers, Jesus must break us open, so we can receive gifts from God. Jesus' love and life don't overcome our need, but flouris' within the openness of our neediness. Human neediness is the openness to heaven's riches.

Second, brokenness brings humility for hearing Jesus. Hearing requires a proper humility about holy things. Proverbs is full of promises whereby God reveals His secrets to the humble, since the high and mighty are only hearing themselves. Isaiah observed that the most teachable and receptive to divine knowledge are those who just "weaned from . . . the breast," i.e., babes (Isa. 28:9). Jesus Himself told the large-and-in-charge leaders that God has "hidden these things from the wise and prudent [but] revealed them to babes" (Matt. 11:25 NKJV).

> *Humilitas pene tota disciplina Christiana est. Almost the whole of Christian teaching is humility.*
>
> —St. Augustine[9]

Third, brokenness brings obedience for hearing Jesus. Jesus said, "If anyone's will is to do God's will, he will know whether the teaching is from God or whether I am speaking on my own authority" (John 7:17 ESV). The willingness to do what is said is necessary for hearing what is said. Why do we fail to hear God speaking? Augustine answered it this way: "Why does [someone] not see God? Because he has not love itself. That he does not see God is because he does not have love; that he does not have love is because he does not love his brother. The reason then why he does not see God is that he has not love. For if he had love, he would see God, for 'love is God.'"[10]

If a person is full of pride and isn't willing to obey what's heard, he or she won't hear (recognize) the Lord. Most of us have been educated far beyond our level of obedience. It's not that we don't know enough, but that we know too much. We think we have God figured out and theologically fastened down. We busy ourselves with so many things for God. We excuse or ignore our weakness and wickedness and spend more and more time wandering in nights of nostalgia and day clouds of disobedience. And we spend less and less time opening ourselves to the wonder and incomprehensible immensity that is God. God's voice is less an intriguing comment than a dazzling comet that drives us to our knees. Jesus' different titles elicit different kinds of responses:

As King, we crown Him.

As Brother, we carry and cover Him.

As Baby, we adore Him.

As Son of God, we revere Him.

As Son of Man, we prefer Him.

As Son of David, we defer to Him.

As Shepherd, we follow Him.

As Rabbi, we learn from Him.

As Last Adam, we honor him.

As Savior, we thank Him.

As Lord, we obey Him.

As Christ, we serve Him.

As Jesus, we love Him.

Once you have heard Jesus, not to obey Him is to betray Him.

The man who is filled with the Holy Spirit speaks in different languages. These different languages are different ways of witnessing to Christ, such as humility, poverty, patience and obedience; we speak in those languages when we reveal in ourselves these virtues to others. Actions speak louder than words; let your words teach and your actions speak. We are full of words but empty of actions, and therefore are cursed by the Lord, since he himself cursed the fig tree when he found no fruit but only leaves. . . .

Happy the man whose words issue from the Holy Spirit and not from himself!

—SAINT ANTHONY OF PADUA (1195–1231)[11]

The truth is that we are not our wounds. The truth is that Jesus can turn our mourning into dancing, our brokenness into beauty, if only we don't block out the Son, the very Son of God. There is still power in the blood of Jesus. Jesus' body was broken for us, so that we might become whole again. By His stripes, by His wounds, we are healed.

Like a Japanese *Kintsugi* bowl—pottery that has been made beautiful by being broken and glued back together with lacquer, then dusted with gold, silver, or platinum—the church bears the wounds of its brokenness. But that brokenness has become exquisite, a precious made-by-the-hand-of-Christ mark clearly upon it. Sealed with the blood of Christ, the church is made beautiful and strong—a baptismal font of blessing to all, a well of Living Water for the well-being of the wounded with an invitation for all to "come . . . and drink" (John 7:37). Jesus bears the wounds of our disobedience, our disbelief, our doubt. To hear Jesus clearly, the church must pick up the pieces of the broken hearts of this world and invite Jesus' golden, shining, enduring love to fill, patch, heal, and mend lives into beautiful, sincere images of God's glory.

The wounds speak. Jesus bears the woundedness of your life and mine upon His body, and He takes those wounds with Him into eternity. Not the scars—the wounds. You touch the Father's mind in Jesus' glorified face. You touch the Father's heart in Jesus' wounded hands and feet. The wounds speak.

Good Heartburn

There's an old Appalachian saying that asks, "Are your ears ringing?" when someone is talking about you. In the case of Cleopas and Mary, it wasn't ringing ears but burning hearts. Even though it didn't register at the time, they began to feel their hearts burning as Jesus spoke to them and told them the story. Jesus started at the beginning and told the whole story, the whole shebang, and how that story is really His story. Because of His story, you and I can be restored and made whole again. We can even be strongest in our most broken places.

Some of us were raised with only negative associations of the word *cholesterol*. Then we learned that there is "good cholesterol." It's the same with heartburn. There are countless medicines promising to cure heartburn, including that chic little purple pill, Nexium. But just as we learned there is good cholesterol, we learn from the Emmaus disciples there is good heartburn.

Whenever we connect, commune, and collaborate with Jesus, there is good heartburn. Our hearts are "warmed" when we experience Jesus' presence and recognize His voice. That is why the Emmaus disciples asked themselves, "Did not our heart burn within us while He talked with us on the road, and while He opened the Scriptures to us?" (Luke 24:32 NKJV). It's a warmth that grows into a fire that burns our hearts to love and service, just as it did John and Charles Wesley. You don't preach 40,000 sermons and travel 250,000 miles on horseback or write 6,500 hymns or publish 5,000 books, tracts, and pamphlets because you are motivated by a tepid, lukewarm, "Laodicean" heart. Only heartburn causes such blow-it-down passion for mission. Only those whose "heart speaks to heart" (*cor ad cor loquitur*) in the silence of the heart are those "in whose heart are the highways to Zion" (Ps. 84:5 ESV).

Jesus' Disappearing Act/Jesus' Present Voice

But wait. As Cleopas and Mary saw the risen Lord, the bodily presence of Jesus disappeared. Once He took His place in their hearts, He disappeared. As He would tell His disciples later in the Upper Room, "It is better for you that I go away" (John 16:7 YLT).

So let's summarize how we hear Jesus speak from what we learned from the Emmaus road story:

- Christ speaks to you in the Scriptures.
- Christ speaks to you in questions.
- Christ speaks to you at table in bread and wine.
- Christ speaks to you in wounds.

And here are the biggest Emmaus surprises:

First, when you invite Jesus into your heart and home, Jesus will always be the host at your table. Your heart will no longer be your own.

Second, as you remember Jesus and recognize His wounds, your own wounds will be healed, and your heart will start beating again.

Unless the eye catch fire
The God will not be seen.
Unless the ear catch fire
The God will not be heard.
Unless the tongue catch fire
The God will not be named.
Unless the heart catch fire
The God will not be loved.
Unless the mind catch fire
The God will not be known.

—ATTRIBUTED TO WILLIAM
BLAKE, "THE FOURFOLD VISION"[12]

Third, comprehending the story is not the same as recognizing Jesus. Cognition is not recognition. It is one thing to keep alive the memory of a dead Jesus. It's a very different thing to hear and obey a living Jesus. Faith is a lifelong Emmaus road journey in hearing and following a living Lord.

Fourth, if you want to keep hearing Jesus, and join Him in what He is already doing, look for the wounds. Let your heart be pierced, so that Jesus' love can pour out for the weak, the wounded, the poor, and the oppressed.

Fifth, once our eyes are opened and our hearing kicks in, our faith takes over. Jesus vanishes from the Emmaus disciples' sight even as their sight is opened and their ears are unplugged.

For the practical application of the themes mentioned
in this chapter, see chapters 16–19 in volume 2.

THREE

The Elusive Voice of Jesus

Jesus' Third Appearance: Jesus Speaks to

His Disciples in a Closed Room

When John, the "beloved disciple," witnessed the empty tomb and the discarded shrouds in Jesus' place of burial, he "saw and believed"—even though he admitted he did not fully understand (John 20:8–9). It is such a comfort that the disciples didn't always understand what Jesus was saying or doing. Yet even when they didn't get it, they stayed with Him and trusted Him, and He them. We don't abandon each other even in our confusion and incomprehension, but we walk together through the fog and mist, the doubts and doldrums.

There were reports of the empty tomb from Mary Magdalene, Joanna, and Mary the mother of James. There was John and Peter's eyewitness experience of the empty tomb. There was the amazing tale of the Emmaus road travelers and their encounter with a risen Jesus. Yet still, Jesus' disciples left behind, the Eleven, remained shuttered and shut down in an obscure upper room in post-Passover Jerusalem. They were afraid and alone, hiding from those who would associate them with the crucified Jesus, "the King of the Jews" (Matt. 27:37 GNT).

Lockdown

John depicted a scary time in a locked-down room somewhere in Jerusalem (John 20:19–31)—a gruesome reminder about the consequences of going against those who hold the reins of power. Who could blame Jesus' disciples for keeping a low profile, for hunkering in the bunker and trying to be as inconspicuous as possible?

This moment of fear was overcome by the mysterious appearance of Jesus—a sudden showing that moved through locked doors and closed minds. Nothing can keep Jesus, "the Door," "the Gate," "the Cornerstone," "the Temple,"[1] out of the inner hearts of His disciples. And nothing prevents Him from entering in different ways than others must. No box can keep Him in—or out.

Jesus appeared to His disciples and embraced them first and foremost with the sound of "Shalom"—"Peace be with you" (Luke 24:36; John 20:19). "Shalom" was a greeting that was traditional and yet, under the circumstances, rejuvenatingly relevant. The Man of Sorrows had become the Man of Shalom.[2]

Jesus' calming voice of "peace" was not just about uncurling from the corner of that locked room. The reflex of reverence and trust over fear and doubt would be a learned response that would challenge the disciples (and us) for the rest of their (and our) lives. Jesus' voice brought to the disciples then, and brings to us today, a peace that is also an empowerment.

It is unclear how many days the disciples gathered as an upper-room mound of mourning, but we know that Jesus appeared to them on the first day, the same day he appeared both to Mary at the tomb and to the two on the road to Emmaus. In the Jewish tradition the death of a family member required a seven-day period of "sitting shivah," a ritualized formal mourning period.

When honoring the dead by sitting shivah, family members stay at home and cover mirrors with cloth in order to not dwell on the physical. There is the tradition of tearing a strip of cloth off one's clothing as a sign of grief and loss, and family members sit on low stools instead of comfortable furniture during the week of mourning. Jesus' "family," His disciples, were certainly sitting shivah for their beloved master/rabbi/ teacher in this shut-off, shut-down space. After the required time of official mourning, the disciples would be free to leave Jerusalem and disperse to their own homes.

But during this official time of mourning, suddenly Jesus appeared in their midst. The first thing He did was declare a message of shalom, or peace. The physicality of the resurrected Jesus was emphasized, as it would be in Luke's gospel, when Jesus invited His disciples to "touch me and see" (Luke 24:39).

He then calmly chowed down on some broiled fish as He joined them for dinner (v. 42). The resurrected Jesus is not a ghost or apparition or holy hallucination. He is the real deal. The life of faith is not life in a fishbowl, or life in a dust bowl, or life in a celebrity/Hollywood bowl, or life in a Super Bowl, but life holding a begging bowl. "Christianity is one beggar telling another beggar where to find bread" when the bowl has run dry.[3] Which is why we meet around the table, as Jesus met with His disciples around a table immediately before His crucifixion, and then again immediately after His resurrection.

The Very Present Jesus Speaks

After table time with His disciples, the risen Jesus gave His followers one last "Bible study." Luke specifies that these Bible lessons Jesus gave came from what is known in Judaism as the *Tanakh*—the Torah (the Teachings), the *Nevi'im* (the Prophets), and the *Ketuvim* (the writings). In other words, Jesus took as His text the whole of the Scriptures as Jesus and His disciples knew them in order to remind them who He was. Here was the whole shebang in one lesson, just as He had given another whole-shebang Bible study to the Emmaus road disciples.

Jesus' lesson was yet another connecting of the dots to show that "the Messiah will suffer and rise from the dead on the third day" (Luke

24:46). Jesus' appearance in their midst affirmed the first part of the scriptural pronouncement: "that repentance and forgiveness of sins should be proclaimed in his name to all nations" (v. 47 ESV). The knowledge of God is greater, not lesser, than the knowledge of the sacred story of the Scriptures. To hear Jesus speak is to know the Scriptures.

Some of us grew up in homes or in churches where we heard people claim, "Thus saith the Lord." In other words, they would often claim "Jesus told me" this and "Jesus told me" that. But the only way to verify whether they were truly hearing an authentic voice of the Lord would be to determine whether their claims were in harmony with the biblical story or if they contradicted it.

The primary voice of Jesus speaking will always be the Scriptures.

Staying Power

While Jesus' first word to His disciples postresurrection was "Peace," His last word to them, according to Luke, was "Stay." There are so many times in life when staying is far harder than leaving:

- staying in school, when it would be so much easier to drop out and get a job—a job that might pay now, but you know won't pay later
- staying as a friend to one who is in trouble and truly troubled
- staying strong when a crisis hits your family—financial, physical, or emotional
- staying with a chronically ill child, spouse, or parent, which is comparable to running a marathon you never got the chance to train for
- staying in ministry when jealous detractors and bullies are spreading outrageous lies about you in an effort to make you quit

"Staying power" is what Jesus requires of us if we are to hear all He has to say to us.

The disciples were given this miraculous news (again!). Yet (again!) there was a period of staying. What we have failed to see in this story is the Jewish background and Jewish rituals of mourning. In traditional Jewish mourning practices, the seven days of sitting shivah are followed by another twenty-three of being removed from everyday life. There is no participation in everyday interactions, in human activities that involve any form of celebration.

Shivah is a time to be quiet, to remember, to reflect inwardly, to "memento mori," to "stay." And that was precisely Jesus' last directive to His disciples: stay in Jerusalem until the Spirit comes upon you (Luke 24:49).

It was the last thing the disciples wanted to hear. It was the hardest thing for them to do. Everything in them wanted to run. But Jesus said, "Stay." Stay here in the very city that killed Me and can come after you. Stay here "until you have been clothed with power from on high" (v. 49). Jesus then led His disciples out to Bethany (a scant two-mile hike) and there "was carried up into heaven" (v. 51 ESV).

Stay. It is sometimes the hardest of directives. But it may be the very thing we need to do the most to hear what Jesus is saying.

The disciples only partly fulfilled this order. You know the disciples, the duh!-ciples, who always did exactly what Jesus told them to do (for example, when He asked them to "stay awake!" in the Garden of Gethsemane and they fell asleep).

Yes, they went back to Jerusalem.

Yes, they probably continued to stay in their safe house, waiting for the "power from on high" that Jesus had promised.

After all, they were caught in an in-between moment: a time when they were supposed to be in mourning, yet a time when they knew they were *not* mourning but rejoicing in a new reality.

A case could be made that they could not resist doing *something.*

So, instead of following Jesus' directive to stay and do nothing until His Spirit released them, they decided to do some bookkeeping. They spent their time not listening and praying, but keeping tabs and filling job descriptions. After the risen Lord ascended to heaven, His followers decided that their most important task was to bring back their number to twelve instead of eleven. The first chapter of Acts is all about the election of this Judas replacement, this new twelfth disciple.

Staying is hard. Staying is not rewarding. Staying does not get you recognition. Staying is . . . staying. Being there. Being in the moment. Champing at the bit. Restraining yourself. Deferring gratification. Putting oneself in a waiting, receiving mode. It is one of the hardest things we ever do in life.

But staying also gives us the freedom to hear Jesus speak. Drop a slab of bacon on the floor and tell your dog to stay. How hard is it? A dog who knows how to stay, who hears the voice of his master and obeys it, even facing a slab of bacon, is a dog that has freedom. Dogs that learn to stay—not just to sit and stay, but to truly listen and obey—are dogs that can go anywhere and do anything. They can go outside without fear. They can go for long walks without leashes. They can always be close to their masters. They can stay close and live close.

Jesus sometimes tells His new family of followers to stay. Even though it may be dangerous to one's personal safety, when Jesus says, "Stay," we stay. Staying is hard. The disciples were mostly country bumpkins not used to hanging out in the city, much less the temple. Yet this was where Jesus instructed them to stay until they received the gift of "Go!"—the empowering presence of the Holy Spirit.

Staying in a place of danger, staying in a place that is fearful and unfamiliar—that is not easy. But Jesus also promised a great gift to those who stayed the course: "I am going to send you what my Father has promised . . . stay in the city until you have been clothed with power from on high" (Luke 24:49).

The gift to those who stayed was the gift of the Holy Spirit. All good things come to those who stay. In your life you will hear the word *go. Go* takes courage and faith. But in your life you will also hear the word *stay,* which takes even more courage and faith sometimes than *go.* But staying the course sometimes requires staying power.

Can you *stay*? *Stay* and *hear* the Lord is good!

Original Kiss, Original Voice

Luke's story ends with Jesus' opening of the Scriptures and instruction to wait to receive the promise of the Father. John, however, tells us that Jesus breathed on His disciples, saying, "Receive the Holy Spirit" (John 20:22), pre-commissioning them in the Upper Room. The emphasis in John is on sending, similar to the mountaintop commissioning found in Matthew (which we will discuss in a later chapter). "As the Father has sent me, I am sending you," Jesus said (v. 21). And again, repeated, "Shalom!" Jesus' breath is Holy Breath, the Holy Breath of God, releasing us into the world as redeemed creatures. Jesus was betrayed with a kiss, but He also redeems the world for God with a "kiss."

Your "first kiss" was the kiss of life breathed into you by the power of the Creator God. That kiss was God's voice speaking you into existence; the first sound you heard was the sound of your divinely gifted humanity, your be-ing as a human. Your first kiss was God's first word to you: "Let there be . . ."

The "first kiss" all living beings receive is the voice of God, the breath of being, the word of life. In the micro-account of the creation of the world (Gen. 2:7), human life comes about because God breathed *"ruach"* into the first human—"the breath of life."[4] It was a kiss of love that extends from the beginning of human existence until today.

And you kissed back. The name of God disclosed to Moses, *ehyeh asher ehyeh*, with its repeated "h" and "sh" sounds, "is as near as we can get in language to pure breath."[5] In other words, with every breath we take, we invoke God's name without moving tongue or lips. We inhale YH (Yah), we exhale WH (weh). Every child's first breath mouths God's name. Every dying person's last breath utters God's name. In fact, every word spoken—for words are carried aloft on breath-wings—speaks the unutterable name of God.

But wait: your remembered "first kiss" of life was not your "second kiss" of everlasting life. The breath that God breathed into the First Adam was not the last breathing of God's love. It was just the beginning.

You know how much you love your children when they are first born. You know how much *more* you love your children when you have cared for them, cried with them, rocked them, and nurtured them for as many years as you are gifted with their presence.

Centuries of God's faithfulness and steadfast mercy toward us, God's children, finally brought God's love to a totally new and wholly redeeming possibility. When the Holy Spirit breathed on Mary and brought Jesus to birth, a renewed "kiss" was bestowed upon humanity. In medieval art, the immaculate conception of Mary was achieved through the ear, as the voice of God radiated from heaven to earth to Mary's receptive ears.

Jesus, the Last Adam, was God's re-kiss of Adam—a kiss of beauty, a kiss of goodness, a kiss of truth. Humanity was no longer "cursed" by our bull-kissing worship of golden calves (cf. 1 Kings 19:18; cf. Hosea 13:2). At Golgotha, the place of the skull, the serpent's skull was crushed and the First Adam's curse was broken (Gen. 3:15). God's re-kiss of humanity with the lifting up of Jesus made possible a whole new relationship with our Creator.

John's gospel starts in the heavens, not on earth: "In the beginning was the *Logos*, and the *Logos* was with God, and the *Logos* was God" (John 1:1). A better translation of *Logos* than "Word" is "Voice" or even "Song." In the beginning was the Song. To hear that song we must stop our worship at the various golden calves that attract us to detract us.

The "Right Stuff" Voice

Because of the dramatic events described in Acts 2, the church celebrates the day of pentecost later in the church year. But what happens next is a proto-pentecost, a promise of what is to come from their "staying" and a replay of the "first kiss."

We usually translate the words in John 20:22 like this: Jesus "breathed on them" and said, "Receive the Holy Spirit." The image is one of Jesus blowing His breath over His frightened followers in this closed-off

34

closeted space. But the breathing that Jesus does is not literally *on* them but *into* them. Only a few days after Judas gives Jesus a kiss-off on the cheek, a betrayal that marked not just Judas but all the disciples, Jesus reverses that kiss and seals His continuing presence with a kiss.

It is a mistake for translators to shy away from the intimacy of inbreathing and kissing by translating the passage "breathed on." Rather, this is the same language of God's breathing in Adam (Gen. 2:7), Elijah and the widow's dead son (1 Kings 17), and Ezekiel's bones (Ezek. 37). Breathing *on* is what we'd do to clean glasses or a mirror. Breathing *into* someone is what we do when we kiss. Jesus breathed into them. God blows God into Adam's nostrils. God creates life out of God's very being/ spirit/breath, out of the divine stuff—the "right stuff."

In other words, the faith of the fearful and frightened was breathed back to life by the resuscitating power of the Holy Spirit—giving them the backbone, the "right stuff" to blow open those locked doors and be the first expression of the church in the world. Jesus' resurrected presence breathed new, enduring life into His disciples, the earnest of the *ecclesia*. Jesus, the Second Adam, breathed the "second kiss"—the kiss of redemption, forgiveness, and eternal life—into these fallen and frail followers.

Jesus' kiss of the Holy Spirit in that little Upper Room, which became a "great kiss" at pentecost, made it possible for His disciples to later step out of that locked-up room and locked-down fear and to go back into the world. Jesus' kiss is a kiss that must be passed on. And every time the gospel is spread, and the good news that Jesus Christ is risen is voiced, we share in that kiss: "For God so loved the world . . ." (John 3:16). Jesus' disciples are those who have been called to kiss the world back to life and forth to love. You are still called to offer this world a kiss, the third kiss that every child of God may receive.

The "first kiss" is the kiss of life, of creation from God the Father.

The "second kiss" is the kiss of redemption and forgiveness from Jesus the Son.

The "third kiss" is the kiss of new life in a new community called the church, the body of Christ, empowered by a personal experience of the risen Christ.

Jesus' "As" Voice

As disciples we gratefully receive those first two kisses. But as disciples we are also called to a lifelong mission to continue to offer that third kiss to the rest of the world. That is why discipleship and evangelism are the same thing. *"As the Father has sent me, even so I am sending you,"* Jesus said (John 20:21 ESV).

As . . . so.

Let's hear the *as* right, and then we'll live the *so* right.

When parents send their young children out to catch the bus, they give them a kiss. When they send their older children off to college or a new home and job, they give them a kiss. When a spouse leaves to go to work or on a business trip, she or he receives a kiss from the husband or wife.

These are not good-bye kisses. These kisses are takeaway meals of love and compassion. We offer a kiss at the doorway with the faith that it is a kiss to a gateway into the world that awaits.

The church has become somewhat stingy with its kisses. Instead of kissing the twenty-first-century culture in which we live and are called to offer the gift of Christ, we play coy and hard to get. Too often the church behaves as though we have the answers, but the world had better come and kiss up to us in order to hear them. Jesus' disciples are supposed to kiss and tell, not to tell and then kiss.

What's the difference? Consider the example of Charley and Sara. Charley and Sara sometimes hang out together, but Charley really doesn't like Sara very much. One day it hits him: *The way to help Sara is to date her! If we were to go out, my strengths could rub off on her, and she would be far better off for it. It will require sacrifice on my part, but it's the least I can do.*

Charley marches up to Sara's door with a book entitled *100 Things*

Sara Needs to Change in Order to Become a Real Person. He rings the doorbell. When she answers, he shoves the book in her face and states, "I've decided it would be best for you if we date. When you finish reading this, I'll be waiting in my truck!"

Charley is Gene Greitenbach's metaphor for the current state of discipleship in our churches today.[6] Charley is not offering to *kiss* Sara. He is *kissing off* Sara and her unique needs and gifts in exchange for a list of "upgrades" he is offering.

Paul urged all Christians to "greet one another with a holy kiss" (2 Cor. 13:12). This uniquely Christian greeting became a kind of secret handshake within the faith community. Among the first generations of Christians, greeting each other with a kiss was a sign of the transmission of the Holy Spirit—its passing on and surpassing power. Following the consecration of the bread and wine, the words spoken were "*pax vobiscum*" ("peace to you"), after which the members of the body of Christ would kiss one another. Thus they became one in the Spirit, enabling them to receive the Eucharistic body of Christ as "one body and one soul" and be incorporated into His Spirit. It was this Spirit-empowered kiss that disciples were to offer to the broken and bleeding world.

The kiss the church has to offer is not like the one we offer to a four-year-old with a boo-boo. It is not a "make it all better" kind of kiss. It is a kiss that makes it all different. It is a kiss of life and love and forgiveness that transforms lives and restores a relationship with God through the power of Christ's sacrifice.

The third kiss is the breath of new life. The third kiss is the sound of the end of the voice of sin and death—and the victory of the powerful, redemptive voice of God.

For the practical application of the themes mentioned
in this chapter, see chapters 20–24 in volume 2.

FOUR

The Challenging Voice of Jesus

Jesus' Fourth Appearance: Jesus Speaks to Thomas

When Jesus breathed the Spirit into His cringing disciples in that room with the bolted door, they became New Adams too. He breathed new life into them with all of the power and authority that suggests. All but Thomas, who wasn't there.

On that first Sunday evening on the day Jesus was found missing from the tomb, the Emmaus road pair reported to "the eleven and those who were with them gathered together" (Luke 24:33 ESV). Thomas was not present when Jesus made His appearance to this group. Perhaps Thomas stepped out for some reason, or just wasn't with them at the time, and "the eleven" was a term used as a general description of the group of disciples once Judas had died. John 20:26 tells us that Thomas had to wait another eight days for Jesus to appear to the group again (KJV).

When Thomas wasn't present (ever wonder where he went?), he missed out on the experience of the risen Christ. Either he was in the wrong place at the wrong time, or he purposely separated himself from the band of disciples. But even though he was not there, the Eleven did not discipline him or scold him or banish him. They held on to him even when he was held in the grip of doubt and disbelief. And when Thomas did come back,

39

he uttered one of the greatest confessions of faith in Jesus in the New Testament: "My Lord and my God" (John 20:28).

When Jesus picked up one child and put that little one on His lap, He picked up all the children of the world. When Jesus let the hemorrhaging woman touch Him, He let all the hemorrhaging people of the world touch Him. When Jesus Himself touched the leper, He touched all the lepers of the world. When Jesus encouraged doubting Thomas to touch Him, He encouraged all the doubters in the world to doubt their doubt.

The Wounds of Doubt

Thomas was not with the disciples in shivah when Jesus first appeared to them. We don't know why Thomas wasn't with his colleagues. For whatever reason, Thomas separated himself from the community. And he missed the moment. He missed hearing Jesus. When you are in despair and doubt, the worst thing you can do is separate yourself from your brothers and sisters in Christ. You see and hear your way to Jesus through the witness of others and in company with them. Don't be so preoccupied with what's missing in your past that you fail to see and nourish your present connections. When you pass through the valley of the shadow (Ps. 23 kjv), lean forward and lengthen the shadow you leave behind. When you "pass through the Valley of Baka [Weeping], . . . make it a place of springs" (Ps. 84:6); make your weeping a well for others to drink from.

> *Melius est dubitare de occultis, quam litigare de incertis: It is better to make doubt of those things which are secret, than to strive about things that are uncertain.*
>
> —AUGUSTINE[1]

When the disciples told the missing Thomas what happened, he insisted on believing the impossible only when he could touch the sword-pierced side and eyeball the wounds. Their words need His wounds,

Thomas says (John 20:19–31). At the end of the week, when Thomas was back sitting shivah with the disciples, Jesus made a special appearance and repeated the first Upper Room scenario, as if just for Thomas.

Speaking directly to Thomas, Jesus said, "Go ahead; here are My hands and feet; put your fingers in My pierced side."

Thomas exclaimed: "My Lord and my God."

We will never know in this life whether Thomas touched Jesus or not.[2] But whether he did or didn't, Jesus invited him to feel free to explore His thorn-pierced brow, nail-scarred hands, spear-thrust side, spike-torn feet.

Both Mary Magdalene and Thomas wanted to touch Jesus' body. Mary was told not to hold on to Him too long; Thomas was told it was okay to touch, but once Thomas could, he perhaps no longer needed to. Jesus doesn't say the same thing to each one of His followers.

Thomas was known as Thomas Didymus, Thomas the Twin, the twin of each of us. Doubt comes with a twin: faith. Like Thomas Didymus, doubt and faith are twinned, always found together. The opposite of doubt is not faith but certainty, which banishes faith. That is why a dollop of doubt is always sprinkled over the seder food, and every person seated at the Passover table is invited to prod and pick at the story of the Hebrews. Sometimes we hear God loudest when the flints are striking together. Faith without doubt is not a living faith, but a dead certainty.

The important thing, anyway, is not knowing how to hear Jesus but actually hearing Him. You can be doctrinally correct, and orthodox to the jot and tittle of the creeds, and still not know Jesus. Or to use the language of my theological ancestors, it is one thing to claim to be a "holiness man" or "holiness woman" and quite another to be a holy man or holy woman.

The Challenge of Faith

Why did Jesus make it a point to visit Thomas after the resurrection? After all, the rest of us didn't get to see the risen Savior standing before

41

us; why should he? Jesus made a special trip just to speak to the one who demanded a sign or proof. Isn't that what every disciple since the first twelve has secretly wished for at one time or another? "Give me, just me, a special word, a personal sign, a secret visit."

There is nothing in the Scriptures to lead one to believe that Thomas would have been treated any differently by the disciples had he never seen Christ resurrected. There is no hint of any exclusion that might have occurred had Thomas not been able to touch the wounds of Christ. There is no reason to claim that such a possibility is even remotely alluded to in the gospel of John—except for human nature . . . and history.

We fallen human beings have a storied, sordid history of executing others because they do not believe as we do. We have burned them, skinned them, drowned them, and excommunicated them. Whether it was because they did not believe the bread was what we thought it to be or because they dunked or sprinkled, we have found reason to believe falsely about the "unbeliever." We have expressed our "us versus them" theories from the political platforms to the playgrounds, excluding people from our group because they were different or didn't believe as we do. Whether it is the colors of a flag we wave or the colors worn by street gangs, we have proven ourselves more than willing to shed blood for the purity of what we believe is the right way things should be done.

Why then would it come as any surprise to consider that Thomas was destined to become the odd man out for being the one disciple who hadn't witnessed the resurrection? Would there not arise at some point in the decisions and discussions between the disciples a certain wonder as to why Jesus never came to see Thomas? Perhaps a blaming of Thomas for not being where he was supposed to be and a lessening of his apostolic authority? Maybe he wasn't worthy. Maybe Jesus knew something they did not. Maybe Thomas's quickness to doubt was an indication of his lack of faith. Jesus' visit silences those voices.

It is only when we recognize this truly human trait of exclusion as a fairly predictable phenomenon that we may understand the miracle of Christ's special visitation to Thomas. The purpose of the visitation was not so much for proof as it was for restoring one back to the community. Thomas eventually would have found his faith in Jesus even if Jesus had not appeared to him personally. But would he ever have found his equal standing with his colleagues? Was it the doubt within Thomas that Jesus was addressing or ultimately the doubt among others about Thomas that Jesus set straight?

Perhaps we'll never really know if this is a valid reading or not, especially if this passage is always interpreted by those who believe that their personal encounter with Jesus is the standard. But for just a moment, let's see the story through different eyes. Let's hear the Master speak to Thomas and challenge him to touch His wounds. And then? What if Jesus turned and looked at the other disciples and stated, "Blessed is the one who believes without seeing" (John 20:29, author's paraphrase)? What if Jesus wasn't directing these words to Thomas, but to the rest of the disciples and to us?

Suddenly it becomes a challenge to the community rather than a chastisement of the individual. It is a request that His followers have enough faith to believe that others may also be disciples without having to witness actual proof every time. Blessed is the church who can believe that the stranger may have followed Christ without his having to speak their faith language. Blessed is the Christian who can hear the heartbeat of God pounding in the life of a doubter and debtor, a "none-er" and a "done-er." Blessed is the one who appreciates the mother who works seven days a week to provide for her family even if she has no energy for hours of service in the church. The voice of Christ beckons to the doubter and challenges the sure.

In one of Franz Kafka's notebooks, there is a dangling, detached comment that sits on the page like a single stick of dynamite: "Religions get lost, as people do."[3] Christianity can get lost, your local church can get lost, just as Thomas got lost. We always get lost when we lose sight of—or leave hearing distance—of Jesus.

Would not the power of hope, faith, and love

There lives more faith in honest doubt, Believe me, than in half the creeds.

—ALFRED, LORD TENNYSON[4]

offered by Christ be so much more earth-shattering had the church grasped that those simple words in the gospel of John were spoken not to an individual who was hurt because he missed out, but to us, to challenge us to not only have faith in the Christ we know, but in the Christ we don't know?

*For the practical application of the themes mentioned
in this chapter, see chapters 25–28 in volume 2.*

FIVE

The Forgiving Voice of Jesus

Jesus' Fifth Appearance: Jesus Speaks to Peter

I'm going fishing."

Peter exclaimed these words (John 21:3 HCSB) as he headed back to fill the void with the familiar, back to the water and the shores of the Sea of Galilee (a.k.a. Sea of Tiberias). Half the disciples (Thomas, Nathaniel, James, John, and two others) dutifully followed him. Once again, Peter led the way. If he wanted to fish, the disciples wanted to join him.

Even though Jesus had already appeared to them twice when they were staying in Jerusalem,[1] the disciples were still confused, bewildered, and unsettled. When Jesus wasn't there with them, it didn't seem real.

Peter in particular was in a free fall and deep funk. Peter had assured Jesus that he had His back, and instead, he stabbed his Lord in the back three times. Jesus obviously knew what Peter had done but hadn't mentioned the cursing or the denying in His Upper Room appearances. Would He? Could Peter ever be trusted by Jesus again? Feeling inadequate, embarrassed, doubting whether he had it in him to be a disciple, Peter ran away.

He ran away from his denials and betrayals. He ran back to what he knew best, back to what he did in his former life. What Peter didn't yet quite get is that God doesn't turn His back on us. It is we who, for whatever reason, turn our backs or don't turn back to God, no matter how much grace God churns out and turns our way.

At night, the seven disciples cast their nets, not to catch the hungry, as Jesus had commissioned them, but to catch fish to sell to the hungry. Fishermen fished when it was dark, so they could sell the fish fresh in the morning. But the fishing disciples found out that they couldn't go back. Their former life no longer existed. They couldn't go back and they couldn't go forward. They were stuck. And their nets were empty.

Jesus Speaks . . . in His "Obey Me" Voice

It was daybreak again. The disciples saw a stranger on the shore. The figure in the distance addressed them as "friends" or "children" (*paidia*), an endearing term but one with authority. Once again, Jesus greeted them with a question. In the mists of the morning, He asked, "You didn't catch anything, did you?" The disciples admitted failure. The voice told them to give it one more chance and cast their nets on the other side of the boat. Thinking the stranger had an elevated view of the water, without asking for any further clarification, they took His recommendation and cast their nets to the right.

They pulled in 153 fish—a "perfect catch," an angler would say: one-third to the boat, one-third to the fishermen, and one-third to the owner of the nets. What significance is the number of fish? Who cares? Well, we care. All true fishermen care. Each individual fish—not just the aggregate—mattered. Each one was a different size

Then in fellowship sweet
we will sit at his feet,
or we'll walk by his side
in the way;
what he says we will do,
where he sends we will go;
never fear,
only trust and obey

—JOHN H. SAMMIS,
"TRUST AND OBEY"[2]

and shape and color. If John, a Jew and a fisherman, counted the fish in a Jewish manner, which is called *gematria*, the number becomes "I Am the Lord Thy God." In Jesus' day, 153 was also the number of the sum of diversity in the Sea of Tiberias and a symbol of the abundance and universality that comes with Jesus.

One reason you know when you hear Jesus' voice is that He insists no one be excluded from God's invitation to the table. The bread on the table is Russian pumpernickel, French baguette, Norwegian *lefsa*, German rye, Armenian pocket, Jewish challah, Italian focaccia, Swedish limpa, Indian chapati, English muffin, Australian damper, Ethiopian injera, Irish soda, Mexican tortilla, Slovakian *vanocka*, Turkish *yufka*. The best representation of God is a table where all God's creatures are seated, eating together, and retelling the Story, all the while laughing, arguing, and eating. The one place we can cease to be an American, cease to be a Methodist/Presbyterian/Baptist/Catholic/Orthodox, cease to be a pastor/teacher/author/student, and be at home and where we are most ourselves: the Jesus table.

> "For I am the LORD thy God, the Holy One of Israel, thy Saviour: I gave Egypt for thy ransom, Ethiopia and Seba for thee."
> —ISAIAH 43:3 KJV

You know it's Jesus' voice when you're being stretched to reach out to those you don't want to, or wish you didn't have to, and go in directions you don't wish to go. Jesus is diffusive of Himself, always moving beyond Himself, always seeing the best in others, most natural when opening up to others. Every word Jesus speaks "vibes" in your ears these tremors of truth: God created you uniquely, loves you unconditionally, forgives you unreservedly, empowers you unbelievably, enfolds you unwaveringly, calls you unpredictably.

The disciples' net should have ripped, but it was another seamless garment that couldn't be torn apart (cf. John 19:23–24). Jesus gives all of us a bigger mission than we can handle, a challenge that will always exceed our abilities and even our ambitions.

What yielded a huge catch of fish? Obedience. Obedience bears fruit. Obedience issues in recognition. Once you're open to new possibilities; once you realize that your way is not the only way, that you can drop your nets and throw them in a different direction than the one you're used to; once you hear God's Word in a different way, the sky is the limit. Trust His voice, and your life will exceed expectations. If you aren't seeing "strange things," you aren't seeing Jesus—strange not in the sense of exotic and esoteric, but in the sense of the unexpected and the familiar made strange.

> *"We have seen strange things today!"*
>
> —LUKE 5:26 NKJV

In the missionary task of "fishing," on your own, you fail. But with Jesus, your "catch" is an overload. Though the disciples are overloaded with confusion, Jesus overloads them with blessing.

And after they obeyed, John told Peter, "It *is* the Lord!" (John 21:7).

Jesus Speaks . . . in His Hosting Voice

Clearly, the power to fish belongs to Jesus. And now the disciples belong to Christ, and only with and through His power can they succeed. The power of Christ is a power not our own.

A "new creature" in Christ is a creature dwelling *coram Deo*, which means "before God." This is the good news of redemption. To be "saved" means that grace, not guilt, lies at the core of your life, enabling you to move past your past and write a new story, a new history. This is the scandal of the good news.

> *The tale is not beautiful if nothing is added to it.*
>
> —TUSCAN PROVERB

God does not forget our pasts but continues to love us in spite of our pasts and in the midst of our perpetuating that past in the present—or in other words, in the midst of our sinfulness.

The soul comes alive when Jesus *moves in and lives in it.*

John recognized Jesus first. Peter trusted John's identification, put on some clothes, jumped into the sea, and swam to shore. Peter was stripped for work, naked under the fisherman's tunic he wore to take off the morning chill. Peter probably tucked it in and tied it up for freedom of movement in the water.

Blind Bartimaeus, when he was healed, threw off his outer garment and sought Jesus. Peter, before he jumped into the water, threw *on* his outer garment. Peter couldn't wait to see Jesus, but he also couldn't yet be vulnerable and naked. What was his standing with his Lord? He couldn't be sure. Peter was still hiding from Jesus because of his broken relationship.

As he swam to Jesus, Peter left the haul to the other disciples, who brought the boat in, dragging the fish. When the disciples came ashore, they found Jesus cooking breakfast, one of the two meals first-century Jews were sure to eat every day. Jesus beckoned His team with some bread and fish and a charcoal fire of coals. "Come and have breakfast," He told them (John 21:12). Jesus invited them to add some of their own fish to the fire, and He would cook it for them.

Jesus was purposely re-creating the setting, even the charcoal fire, around which Peter had earlier denied Jesus. Peter's restoration was done before the disciples, so that there could be no question of Jesus' forgiveness. Jesus not only reconciled with Peter in the context of a meal but gave Peter his commission to be bread and go fish while sharing fish and bread.

It was Peter whom Jesus sent back to get more fish to add to what He was already cooking. Peter must participate in the haul, and more than that, be the one who brought the fish to the fire. Jesus primes the pump, starts the pot, but invites us to bring our gifts to make stone soup. A potlatch mission is launched by a potluck meal.

Peter went back to what he knew best. But Jesus spoke and welcomed all of them back to what they knew best together: fishing for and feeding people.

Jesus served the disciples. He anticipated their needs. Scripture doesn't say that Jesus ate, just that He served His disciples and met their hunger. When Jesus speaks, we serve others, anticipating the needs of the world.

Jesus is the host, both of the bread and the fish. We are the guests—guests of each other, guests of life, always and everywhere, on this crowded planet.

God expected Adam and Eve to walk with Him. Adam's sin was that he wasn't walking with God. "If we live in the Spirit, let us also walk in the Spirit," Paul wrote (Gal. 5:25 NKJV). We were made to "walk in the Spirit." Walking in harmony with our Creator enables us to walk in harmony with all creatures and with creation itself. Worship is what you do when you've heard Jesus speak. A worship life is what you live when you walk with Jesus.

There are many ways of serving Jesus. One is to cast yourself into the sea and hurtle headlong into the future, as Peter did. Another way is to stay in the boat and bring the fish to shore, as the disciples did. Another way is to cook the food, or serve the tables, or attend the fishing party with prayers and devotions from the home front. We each hear the same voice but are assigned different missions. Not one is better than the other.

Jesus Speaks . . . in His Do-Over Voice

Jesus gave Peter's calling and calling out a do-over. Around a fire, Peter betrayed Jesus three times. Around this fire by the sea, Peter had three questions to undo before Jesus could reinstate him. In Near Eastern custom, no contract was taken seriously unless it had been reiterated three times before witnesses. But this was unlike any other contract: here the litmus test was love.

Some scholars minimize the difference between Jesus' two uses of *agapao* and one use of *phileo*. We could not disagree more. There is the further question of, what are the "more than these" in Jesus' question "Do you love me more than these?" (John 21:15) Are the "more than these" more than these fish, more than your profession, more than your making a living? Or maybe "more than these" could also mean "Do you love Me more than these other disciples do?" or "Do you love the Shepherd more than the flock?"

It was always dangerous to have a conversation with Peter, for whom speaking was a mode of thinking. So that Peter would not get lost in the mist of his own hot air, Jesus organized their conversation around three missional directives conveyed in carefully chosen metaphors. Jesus chose His metaphors carefully, and so must we. Metaphors are the life-blood of thought. We become the metaphors we choose to live and use to tell the stories of our lives. Encode the stories, encode the metaphors, encode the words of Jesus, and you encode Jesus.

Peter was being encoded with metaphors that would shape the disciples' ministry for the remainder of their days, and ours:

"Tend My lambs" (v. 15 NASB)

"Feed My sheep" (v. 16 KJ21)

"Shepherd My flock" (v. 17, author's paraphrase).

Notice how Jesus defined ministry with verbs, not nouns. Jesus' voice reminds us whose flock it is: not ours, but His.

As they were eating, Jesus addressed Peter directly. When Jesus first met Peter, He called him Simon bar Jonah. Jesus then nicknamed him Cephas (Aramaic, *Kephas*) or Petros (Greek). Now Jesus addressed him as Simon bar Ionanou (John), the name he had when he was first called to discipleship. Why did Jesus revert back to Peter's former, formal name?

The Lord may give you bread of adversity and water of affliction,
but he who teaches you shall no longer be hidden out of sight,
but you with your own eyes, you shall see him always. If you
stray from the road to right or left, you shall hear with your own
ears a voice behind you saying, "This is the way; follow it."

—ISAIAH 30:20–21, AUTHOR'S PARAPHRASE

Jesus was forcing Peter to come to terms with his past, to not block the enormity of his betrayal or the truth of who he is. Peter had to pass through his woundedness to be called back into a renewed relationship with Jesus. Peter was too strong to follow Jesus. He wasn't weak enough to graduate from the school of love. We track the mind of God in the footsteps of Jesus; we touch the Father's heart in the wounds of the Son. The wounded Christ was opening up a festering wound, forcing Peter to face his woundedness so he no longer had to live there but could find his home in the wounds and weakness of love.

There are five thousand wrecks lying deep and undisturbed in the Great Lakes.[3] Every life has wreckage lying beneath the surface, some far down, some not so far. We are all wounded, and we all are wounded in different places and at different depths. In medieval legend, the five wounds of Jesus on the cross stood for His five senses and for the totality of our woundedness—wounds of touch, sight, hearing, scent, and taste. To live in Christ is to participate in His woundedness. At the Lord's Table, Christ inserts His wounded body into ours, so that our bodies might be joined with Him and with others.

Jesus' invitation to Thomas to insert his hand into the wound of God was repeated here in Jesus' sticking of Peter's face in his betrayal of his Lord. Are you afraid to touch your wounds? Are you afraid to touch the wounds of others? The only way to be a disciple is to touch the bleeding, bruised, broken wounds of the world. We want God to work through our channels, to use our means, to meet our deadlines, to fulfill our expectations, to occupy our situations. But God's mission is played out through the logos logic of wind, waves, and wounds—we can't see from whence they come, or where they go, or what bended brokenness in the world truth must pass through and heal.

Once again, Jesus began their conversation with a question: "Do you *agapeo* Me?" In other words, "Do you love Me sacrificially, unconditionally? Do you love Me as God loves?"

Peter responded honestly: "I *phileo* You." In other words, "I will always be Your friend."

"Tend My lambs," Jesus then replied. The word for "tend" is the word used for feeding large flocks of young animals in every kind of pasture.

Jesus tried again: "Do you *agapeo* Me?"

Peter repeated his earlier profession of faith: "I *phileo* You . . . I am Your friend, Jesus."

"Feed My sheep," Jesus responded this time. The word *pomaino* means "to shepherd flocks of sheep." Nurture all the sheep, Jew and Gentile, and do so with a personal touch. In spring, you take the young lambs of winter into the world to become strong and grow through spring and summer.

Jesus gave Peter one last try. Peter was saddened Jesus had to ask him a third time. And Jesus was even sadder that Peter could only "friend" him. It is Jesus who has the right to call us friends, not we who have the right to call Jesus friend.

Peter could only sing "What a Friend I Have in Jesus." Jesus was hoping that Peter could sing "My Jesus, I Love Thee, I Know Thou Art Mine" or at least "O Love That Will Not Let Me Go."

But Jesus "humbled" Himself to bless Peter's best and adopted Peter's word for "love," which is *phileo* or "brotherly love."

"Do you *phileo* Me?"

"Lord, You know I do."

Jesus gave one final charge: "Shepherd My flock." Before rain brings new life in the fall and winter, food must be carried to the sheep as they bear lambs of the spring. The shepherd must be doubly caring, because of all the pregnancies. Jesus was telling His disciples to take care of the sheep through all seasons of life, from youth to old age. Jesus ended His exchange with more pastoral responsibility of sheep than evangelistic obligation of lambs.

Jesus' final words to Peter, "Follow Me" (v. 19 NKJV), do not mean "Take a private walk with Me," but "Follow Me to the cross and beyond." Just after being told that his life would end with a similar fate as that of Jesus, Peter wanted to know about John: "What about him?" (John 21:21). Jesus said that both of them were called to follow Him and to live under the shadow of the cross. For one it means one thing, and for the other it means another. What we are all called to do is follow Jesus, to make a choice to live under God's shadow. To live your life under the shadow of the cross is the path to paradise.

Jesus Speaks . . . in His Forgiving Voice

If you have lived in snowy regions of the world, you know what freezing temperatures can do to the extremities of the body. Maybe you had to change a tire in a snowstorm. Maybe you delivered newspapers as a teenager in subzero temperature. You would return home with hands or ears so frozen they were numb of feeling. It was only when the warmth of the kitchen began to unthaw your ears, or you began rubbing your hands together to bring your shivering stumps back to life, that the pain became excruciating. The more the blood rushed back, the worse the pain became. The hurt evidences healing, a corpse returning to life with blood beneath the skin once again.

> *"Take heed how you hear."*
>
> —Luke 8:18 NKJV

When God's voice of forgiveness starts to warm our hearts and excite the blood, as it did for Peter, the pain is almost unbearable. As our souls unfreeze, our spirits shriek from the horror of our waywardness and the desperation of our contrition. The word *contrition* comes from *tritura*, the rubbing of things together—the rubbing of our hands together to restore warmth, the rubbing "as in the threshing of grain, breaking the outer, inedible husk. So contrition is the threshing of our hearts, softening them, breaking down the hard husks of our hearts, making them hearts of flesh, able to feel sorrow and joy."[4]

A soft heart and a receptive spirit do more to open us to the voice of Jesus than all the disciplines and routines, the works and exercises of conventional piety. Jean-Pierre de Caussade, in a letter to a nun, warned against the "hectic piety" of spiritual disciplines and the studied attachment to interior or bodily devotional "practices":

Believe me, you have too many practices already. What is needed is rather a progressive inner simplification. Too many people identify spiritual prowess with being perpetually busy heaping meditation upon meditation, prayer upon prayer, reading upon reading instead of learning from the simple souls the great secret of knowing how, from time to time, to hold yourself back a little in peace and silence, attentive before God.[5]

Worse still, it encourages people to place their trust in their own good works, instead of in the mercy of God and the merits of Christ—which is nothing but self-love and pride. We can come to be as dangerously attached to our own will in matters of piety and holiness as we can in worldly things, and such pious pigheadedness is still self-love, however spiritualized. Nothing is more contrary to the Spirit of God than this kind of hidden, probably unconscious, vanity, which makes us rely more on our own minds and resolutions and willpower than on God's grace, and which lures us all unaware into telling ourselves complacently how much we are doing for God, for our salvation, for perfection.

This desire for reassurance that we are spiritually in good shape springs simply from self-love. Like worldly worshippers of their own beauty, we want to be able to admire ourselves in our spiritual looking glasses. We attach ourselves to all that can be felt and recognized as holy in ourselves. But really this preoccupation with ourselves is uncalled for, especially the preoccupation with locating exactly our own supernatural status.

The more we become aware of our limitations and insufficiencies, like Peter, the more we are aware of Jesus' voice. The more we recognize how hard of hearing we really are, the more we attune ourselves to hear Jesus' voice. The more we factor in the itchiness and tetchiness of our ears, the more we will hear Jesus speaking. Like a child frustrated by the constraints of crawling who pushes forward to walk, so we push harder in desire and delight to receive the whole message of Jesus.

The sufficiency of our hearing Jesus is not in our skills and expertise and good intentions; the sufficiency is in God. Too often our delight is less in the Lord than in our religious practices and our procured skills at sacred acts and disciplines. The ultimate satisfaction is not in our sufficiency, but in God's sufficiency, and our bare, naked faith in God.

When Christ is present, it's not a religion that is present. When you step into the presence of Christ, you aren't stepping into an organized religion or ritual system or set of spiritual practices. You're stepping into a "real presence" relationship with the very Son of God. The more we are the Presence of Christ for others, the more present we are for Christ to speak to us. We are no longer driven by necessity but by desire and delight. Or as the fifth-century father Saint Gregory of Nyssa taught, "Such was each of the saints who brought himself to God without being compelled."[6] Faith is a relational category requiring relational content and capacities. Christian faith has no meaning outside Christ as its subject, verb, and object.

For the practical application of the themes mentioned
in this chapter, see chapters 29–33 in volume 2.

SIX

The Blinding Voice of Jesus

Jesus' Sixth Appearance: Jesus Speaks
to Paul on the Road to Damascus

Then last of all He was seen by me also,
as by one born out of due time.
—PAUL (1 COR. 15:8 NKJV; CF. ACTS 9:1–9)

Jesus Speaks . . . in His Seeking Voice

One of the biggest obstacles to hearing Jesus speak is the fact that we're in hiding. Ever wonder why moon helmets had one-way mirrored visors? If aliens were found on the moon, they couldn't see the human face. Humans want to remain hidden.

We are especially hiding from the one true God. In fact, the Bible is a hide-and-seek story. But the one seeking is God, and we are the ones hiding. We need "hider-sensitive" worship. We are not created to hide from God but to hide in God. Prayer is not a hideout. Prayer is an acknowledgment of our hidebound dependence on God. When God does play hide-and-seek with us, God hides in order to be more deeply found. God hides for us to more deeply discover God and hear God. The lowest point of God's absence (the cross) becomes the highest point of God's speaking.

Sometimes our very anxiousness about searching for God and straining harder to hear God's voice is what prevents us from hearing God in the first place. Maybe we ought to stop searching for God and instead come out of hiding and let God find us. The best hearing begins with our coming out of hiding and saying to the Great "I AM": "Here am I, Lord."

One of the great hide-and-seek stories of history is the Damascus road story. If ever there were evidence that Jesus comes to us, that Jesus comes to get us, that we are the hounded, the haunted, the hunted, it is the Damascene moment. Every postresurrection appearance of Jesus is at the initiative of Jesus. We have a God who comes to us.

On the road to Damascus, a Seeking God and Interrupting Voice knocked Saul (soon to be known as Paul) off his "high horse" and turned his world upside down. Once you've heard Jesus call your name, you fall on your knees, proclaim Jesus "Lord," get up a changed person (even your name is new), and choose new paths.[1] And then you travel—like the wise men—"by a different route" (Matt. 2:12 PHILLIPS). You also allow yourself to be a sign for others on their journeys.

Were the events in Acts 9 on the road to Damascus all but a dream? Dreams do riddle the biblical drama, and Jesus' voice is often heard in dreams. The Christmas and Epiphany stories began with dreams. But not this one. While Jesus' appearance to Paul may have been different in character from the rest of Christ's pre-ascension appearances, this encounter with Paul was no merely subjective vision or dreamy state, as both Jesus' voice (Acts 9:7) and the bright light (Acts 22:9) were perceived by Paul's traveling companions.

Not every change of heart need resemble a heart attack. Not every "word of the Lord" bowls us over and sends us reeling. Sometimes the loudest quiet comes from the quieting of the loudest places.

When you hear Jesus speak, however, you hear Jesus speak, and there is only one reply. It was the initial and immediate response among the disciples to the appearance of the risen Christ. One word: *Kyrie* or "Lord."

Kyrios (Lord) is a divine title, the title of the Roman emperor. Followers of Jesus refused to say, "*Kyrios Kaisar*," for that is to say yes to the emperor's divinity. Only Jesus was given the divine title *Kyrie*.

"The Lord is risen indeed, and has appeared to Simon!" (Luke 24:34 NKJV).

"It is the Lord" (John 21:7).

"'Saul, Saul, why are you persecuting Me?' And he said, 'Who are You, Lord?'" (Acts 9:4–5 NKJV).

The Easter message was greeted with "*Kyrie*"—"Lord."

When you hear Jesus speak, answer like Samuel, as instructed by his mentor, Eli: "Speak, LORD, for Your servant hears" (1 Sam. 3:9 NKJV). Even Paul, who was blinded and left on the ground, dazed and confused, could only say, "Who are you, Lord?"

Every road you're on can be a road to Damascus, a road to "*Kyrie*-Lord."

The first confession of the church—"Jesus is Lord" (Rom. 10:9; 1 Cor. 12:3).

Jesus Speaks . . . in His Blinding Voice

Faith is "the substance of things *hoped for*, the evidence of things *not seen*" (Heb. 11:1 NKJV). What kind of evidence is that—*not seen* evidence? What kind of faith is that—*hoped for* substance? Paul learned both the hard way on a hard Damascus road.

We hear best when we are transparent, just as glass is transparent. The making of glass dates back thousands of years BC, but it makes an appearance at the beginning of history. In Genesis, we were created from sand mixed with other elements from the ground,

> *Our whole business then, Brethren, in this life is to heal the eye of the heart whereby God may be seen.*
>
> —AUGUSTINE[2]

and water. Glass is made from sand mixed with other elements from the ground, and water, and sodium carbonate (baking soda).

After the fall, we hid ourselves. The glass shattered. We were no longer transparent to God, to ourselves, to each other, to creation. Our eyes were clouded over, muddy, and soiled. Jesus makes new eyes, with mud heated by the fires of the Holy Spirit. He did this with His spit to the blind man of Bethesda (Mark 8:23; John 9:6), and He did this with Paul on the Damascus road. When we experience Jesus' touch and hear His voice, we are brought into the light. To be brought into light, when light can shine through you, you are revealed and redeemed and become a child of the Light. Your glass is re-blown. As a child of the Light, you are given new glasses, new eyes, transparent to the truth, transparent for all to see. To be redeemed is to be revealed.

Before the blinding voice, Paul was like a torch, which shone with his own light. Here was a man with a life rich in privilege, pedigree, power, zeal, scholarship, and Torah-true righteousness. Paul knew "chosenness." First, he was a Jew, a member of a nation chosen by God to be in unique relationship with God. Second, within this Jewish identity, Paul was a Pharisee. Among the chosen, Paul was chosen to wield special power and influence, because of his vast learning and piety. Third, in addition to his chosen-chosen status, Paul also enjoyed unique political status. He was a Roman citizen, and that honor laureled him with rights and privileges that accrued to the most powerful entity on earth at the time—the Roman Empire.

Deeply layered in chosenness, Paul started down the Damascus road with a mission: to round up and haul to Jerusalem followers of a guy named Jesus. Jesus was giving the Pharisees a bad name, because he was so close to them in his training but so far from them in his theology and missiology. Jesus extended God's chosenness to everyone. Even though the Torah commands on thirty-six occasions to love the stranger, the extension of covenantal chosenness to the Gentiles was total heresy for the triply chosen Paul.

New Testament fights between Jews and Christians were "*intramural*" fights, like that in the past between the Protestants and Catholics, or Shia and Sunni in Islam today. Jesus was a Jew, and the biblical fights were fights between Jews about a Jew and over Jewish issues even when they were about Gentiles. There were no "Christians" in the New Testament until Antioch, and even then, they were known as followers of a Jew named Jesus.

What made Paul such a troublemaker after the Damascus road "hearing" was less his opposition to the legalism of a salvation earned by following every jot and tittle of the Law. The Judaism of Jesus' day considered Torah obedience an expression of gratitude for God's choice of Israel and as a badge of fidelity to the covenant.

Paul cannot technically be called the first missionary to the Gentiles. Long before Paul's encounter on the Damascus road, Jesus had sent a missionary to proclaim the good news to the Gentiles: the Gerasene demoniac (Luke 8:26–39). But once Paul understood that Jesus extended God's promises to Abraham and the Jewish people to the whole human race, he developed a missionary theology. Covenant election was open to Gentiles without circumcision. Plus the status of the One through whom that election was possible threatened traditional Jewish monotheism. The only form of chosenness that mattered was that Jesus had chosen Paul to be His disciple. This was the ultimate in chosenness. And it was available to anyone.

Chosenness now had a double meaning. Despite all Paul's prior chosenness—as a Jew, a Pharisee, a Roman citizen—he was really only chosen for death. First, the life lived "to the flesh" (Rom. 8:12) is nothing more than a death march. Second, as one reborn in the Spirit, there is still a death decision that must be faced every day—namely to "put to death," or to mortify, the "deeds of the body" (v. 13 ESV). Only those who have received the Spirit have this death-defying ability. Only those baptized by water and of the Spirit are able to "put to death the deeds of the body" day in and day out.

What has happened to make this possible is an essential change in those who have received the gift of the Spirit. Paul asserted that these are no longer just men and women faithfully following Christ. Those who have Christ's Spirit are now fully "children of God" (v. 14). This new identity is the life-affirming, flesh-transcending chosenness that Paul would come to claim and celebrate. All that Paul had been born into; all that Paul had achieved through study and hard work; all the righteousness Paul had tallied up by doing the right things: all were now but gall to Paul.

After Jesus' blinding voice on the Damascus road, a blazing torch turned into a heap of ashes. Paul was no longer like a torch but a diamond, that brilliantly reflected a borrowed light; without its source, the diamond would be nothing but a dead stone. As he told the Philippians (3:4–14), all the advantages and accomplishments he had in his pre-Damascus life were but "garbage" (v. 8). One day on a Damascus road, Paul suddenly found himself at zero— even less than zero! A flash of blinding light, a heavenly voice, and all accounts were transferred from one side of Paul's life-ledger to the other. The only thing that mattered to Paul now? The fact that he knew Christ.

> *"If therefore the light that is in thee be darkness, how great is that darkness!"*
>
> —JESUS (MATT. 6:23 KJV)

Playwright Samuel Beckett's favorite quote was one he believed to be from Augustine. Beckett used the quote in his television play *Quad* (1981) as well as in one of the most famous plays in history, *Waiting for Godot* (1948):

> Do not despair—one of the thieves was saved;
>
> do not presume—one of the thieves was damned.

There are two things wrong with this. First, Augustine never said it.[3] Two, it's not true. We have assurance of faith to the point where we can "presume." Once Paul heard Jesus speak, he could proclaim for the rest of his life, "I know whom I have believed and am persuaded that He is able to keep what I have committed to Him until that Day" (2 Tim. 1:12 NKJV). Jesus' voice brings assurance.

We must bring the total Christ, not just the historic Jesus, to bear on the totality of our human lives. The historic Jesus cannot save; only the living Christ can save. For Paul, and for us, the historic Jesus must become the living Christ if we are to hear Jesus' voice. Once you are voice-activated, light leaches out of each encounter. But the journey of sanctification is to move from leaking the light to shining the light. The spirit of a disciple is the candle of the Lord, who is the Light of the World.

> *Life is a great bundle of little things.*
>
> —OLIVER WENDELL HOLMES[4]

Jesus Speaks . . . in His Mentoring Voice

The voice of Jesus speaking comes from both without and within. And it's the same voice. But as far as we know from the accounts in the Gospels, Jesus appeared in person after His resurrection only to those who had known Him. Not one physical appearance occurred before this to a non-disciple. Jesus "appeared" to Paul in a blinding voice and through an unsuspecting intermediary, Ananias. The Jewish philosopher and rabbi Emil Fackenheim, who was arrested by the Nazis on the night we know as *Kristallnacht*, contended that if an agnostic had been present at Mount Sinai, he would have heard the thunder and seen the lightning but wondered what all the commotion was about.[5]

To hear the voice of God, you need to be in a relationship with God. Even a negative, argumentative relationship is better than no relationship. The sheep, whether black or white, recognize the Shepherd's voice.

Russian novelist Vladimir Nabokov could not open and close his own umbrella. Other people had to help him.[6] It is not just artists and academics who are notoriously helpless around the mundane matters of life. Football players can't squirt their own Gatorade in the middle of a game. Coaches have to help them.

But all of us need help in life for one thing or another, and one of the hardest things for humans to do is to say, "I need some help." Helping others is not a hobby or a mere helping hand; service is an act of holiness, the privilege of a heritage and the reward of an inheritance as heirs of Christ. Mentoring is one of the highest forms of service.

Paul needed help to hear God. He needed a mentor, an instructor. Learning Christ is discipleship; learning about Christ is scholarship. The former is the way of an apprentice with a mentor; the latter is the way of an academic with a mentor. Both discipleship and scholarship require mentors.

You've heard talk about "sweet surrender"? There's nothing sweet about it. Paul had to be blindsided and go blind to reality to hear the truth. His vision was so self-focused, his hearing so self-absorbed, he needed to be blinded before he could "see," and deafened so he could hear. Plus he needed someone to guide him from darkness to light, from deafness to hearing.

The only thing we know about Ananias is that he was a respected member of the fledgling followers of Jesus at Damascus, the very group Paul was bound and determined to persecute. And Ananias was attuned enough to Jesus' voice to hear it, trust it, and follow it. Although he did register a bit of concern: "You do know, God, that this guy You want me to make an apprentice is the one and same person who is coming here to persecute us, right?"

God is like the sun: never experienced or known directly but only through mediators, intermediaries, agents. God is not hiding, but God is divine, and we are human. God's holiness is supreme. The ancient Hebrews knew a God who was distant and different, but at the same time close, responsive to petitions, and a God who intervened on their behalf. How is God active in the world? Through the Spirit. God is holy and God is here. To reach "here," a God very different from "here" raises up emissaries, intermediaries like Ananias, and releases the Spirit in and through them.

Paul's personal appetite had been for success. He was a scholar, a Roman citizen, a respected Pharisee. His appetite for success had been sated and satisfied. But Paul's desire, his longing for personal redemption, had still been unfulfilled until he met Jesus on the Damascus road. It was only after Paul's mentoring by Ananias, which translated the blinding voice into the language of his life, that Paul realized the satisfaction of his previous appetites had nothing to do with soul satisfaction. It was only after Ananias guided Paul in his stroke of insight that Paul felt the desires of his earthly life find their true fulfilment in the love of God and the love of others. It wasn't that Jesus directly healed Paul. It was Paul's mentor (Jesus through Ananias) who healed him: "The Lord has sent me . . . ," Ananias told him, "so that you may recover your sight" (Acts 9:17 PHILLIPS). Immediately Paul could see.

Jesus said, "I am the vine; you are the branches" (John 15:5). But the vine needs the branches to bear fruit. The same life flows through both. Through Christ we become "partakers of the divine nature" (2 Peter 1:4 NKJV), which means in Christ we are greater than we know. This is what the mentoring voice of Jesus taught Paul:.

> *Things don't satisfy,*
> *because you are greater than things.*
> *People don't satisfy,*
> *because you are greater than people.*
> *Success doesn't satisfy,*
> *because you are greater than success.*
> *Institutions don't satisfy,*
> *because you are greater than institutions.*

There is within you a yearning for the divine that nothing else can satisfy. Your spirit transcends every fortune, every fame, every person who crosses your way. Nothing satisfies, because of your eternal longings that have no earthly resting places. Only Jesus satisfies. Only the One Greater-Than-Everything can satisfy all life's greater-thans. The mentoring voice of Ananias taught Paul what it means that "Jesus Is All the World to Me."

Discipleship formation is nothing more, nor less, than a community where everyone is an Ananias and everyone is being Ananias-ed. In other words, everyone is a mentor in hearing Jesus speak, and everyone has a mentor in hearing Jesus speak.

A blind monk walked with a pupil in a monastery garden on a beautiful spring day. The garden was coming to bloom, and the wind blew softly. As they passed near a large peach tree, the teacher moved his head in order to miss the overhanging limbs.

The pupil looked startled and asked, "Teacher, how is it that you saw those limbs?" The blind monk answered, "To see with the eye is only one sensation. I heard the wind sing softly in the tree's branches."

The pupil looked puzzled as the blind monk continued. "Close your eyes and tell me what you hear. Do you hear your heartbeat? Do you hear the footfall of the monk across the courtyard? Do you hear the grasshopper at your feet?"

The young pupil looked down in astonishment and saw the first grasshopper of the new spring. "How do you hear these things?" the pupil exclaimed.

The blind monk answered, "How do you *not* hear them?"

We all need guides and mentors to help us hear the voice of Jesus. We are all part of a communion of saints: some who are here with us in the here and now, and others who have heard Jesus' voice before us in the past and can help us know how to hear Him today.

We must learn to honor our teachers and mentors. Our forebears in faith must have voice and vote, even an honored seat at the table, in the community of which we are now a part.

It was Ananias's mentoring voice that enabled Paul to be one of the three most influential writers in the ancient world on the human condition: Plato, Paul, and Augustine of Hippo.

It was Ananias's mentoring voice that enabled Paul later to engage

Aeschylus and Epimenides, and mentoring voices that enabled Aquinas to engage Aristotle, Dante to engage Virgil, John Wesley to engage Isaac Newton, you to engage . . . ?

Our greatest mentors may not be living. Our ancestors talked about the *sensus fidelium*, the sense of the faith, the giving of voice and vote to our forebears in faith, even according them the most honored seats at the table. Just when we get discouraged, down, and dumbfounded, there "steals on the ear the distant triumph song . . . and hearts are brave, again, and arms are strong."[7] Some of the best mentoring is done by the gathered community, especially those ancestors who have developed astonishing muscles of the soul. We need to be in a mentoring relationship with Ignatius, Clement, Polycarp, Augustine, Aquinas, Luther, Calvin, Wesley, Jonathan Edwards, Teresa of Avila, A. W. Tozer, T. Austin-Sparks, F. B. Meyer, Watchman Nee, and others.

But it is not just the finest spirits of the past, "For All the Saints," who enable us to live out of their past without living in their past. Church historian Jaroslav Pelikan said, "The history of tradition requires that we listen to the choruses and not only to the soloists—nor only to the virtuosi among the soloists."[8] We also need to be mentored by Romanos the Melodist, Amadeus of Lausanne, Guerric d'Igny, Ephrem the Syrian, Jacob of Serugh, Isaac of Nineveh, and Symeon the New Theologian.

Jesus Speaks . . . in His Suffering Voice

Paul learned on the Damascus road that the true weapons of faith are the wounds of Christ. The wounds of Jesus teach us two important truths:

1. The wounds speak of His sacrifice.

By His death, Jesus paid the ultimate sacrifice for us: His own life. When we hear Jesus speak to us today, what He says will be marked by sacrifice and self-denial.

"Anyone who loves their life will lose it, while anyone who hates their life in this world will keep it for eternal life." (John 12:25)

"Whoever wants to be my disciple must deny themselves and take up their cross daily and follow me. For whoever wants to save their life will lose it, but whoever loses their life for me will save it." (Luke 9:23–24)

Only Christianity answers the question of suffering with a divine experience, not a doctrine or philosophy of suffering. The shadow of the cross is a paradox: the end of suffering comes through suffering. In medicine, this is called the *homeopathic* remedy for disease: the sin of nailing the Messiah to a tree is the redemption of sin. Or as Nicholas Buxton put it:

Brought low, he was raised up. In defeat he was victorious. Through death comes new life. In giving up the "I," emptying the self of itself—as Jesus did on the cross—the self is truly fulfilled. The sign of the cross represents an "I" crossed out, following the self-emptying way of Christ leads not to our obliteration—we will not perish, but have eternal life—for by giving up our false selves we come into the perfect fullness of being that is God.[9]

Jesus wants us to reach out and understand each other, not from the outside in, as the world does, but from the inside out. What makes us think that we can be *with* those who suffer, and be *for* those who suffer, and not suffer ourselves? Suffering without God is a godless misery. Suffering with God is a godly mercy.

2. *The wounds speak of giving.*

For God so loved the world that He *gave* His Son to die for us. When we hear Jesus speak to us today, what He says will be marked by giving to others.

"So in everything, do to others what you would have them do to you, for this sums up the Law and the Prophets." (Matt. 7:12)

Both sacrifice and giving characterize the life of Jesus, which is embodied in the word *love*. Simply put, love is benefitting others (giving) at the expense of ourselves (self-sacrifice).

Other humans in history may have suffered physically more than Jesus, but no human in history loved more than Jesus, forgave more than Jesus, or gave more than Jesus. If you trace the steps of Christ while He was on earth, the common thread behind all that He did was His giving to alleviate human suffering.

God whispers to us in our pleasures, speaks to us in our conscience, but shouts to us in our pain.

—C. S. LEWIS[10]

He comforted the oppressed, rebuked the oppressors, healed the sick, saved the lost, restored sight to the blind, set free the captives.

> "The Spirit of the LORD is upon Me,
> Because He has anointed Me
> To preach the gospel to the poor;
> He has sent Me to heal the brokenhearted,
> To proclaim liberty to the captives
> And recovery of sight to the blind,
> To set at liberty those who are oppressed;
> To proclaim the acceptable year of the LORD." (Luke 4:18–19 NKJV)

Today, Jesus is doing the same thing through you, through us.

He's still sacrificing Himself and giving to those in need, from the least in society to your own blood kin.

We'll give a very simple story.

A young man in his teens began following the Lord wholeheartedly. He asked Jesus to begin speaking to him.

Not long after, his mother was washing the dishes and the thought came to him, *Help your mother wash the dishes.*

The young man didn't like washing dishes, but he recognized the thought to have come from the Lord. What he heard was marked by giving and self-denial.

That small and admittedly basic experience was this man's introduction to a lifelong walk of recognizing the voice of Christ.

So look for the wounds, for therein you will find the voice of Jesus speaking to you.

When Jesus said, "Come, follow Me," He called us to . . .

- come to the sinks and sinkholes of our world.
- come to the soup kitchens.
- come to the homeless.
- come to the bedside of the dying.
- come to the prisoner.
- come to the cross.

For the practical application of the themes mentioned in this chapter, see chapters 34–42 in volume 2.

SEVEN

The Missional Voice of Jesus

Jesus' Seventh Appearance: Jesus' Ascension

Then the eleven disciples went away into Galilee, to the mountain which Jesus had appointed for them. When they saw Him, they worshiped Him; but some doubted.
—MATTHEW 28:16–17 NKJV

Jesus Speaks . . . in His Mountain Voice

Jesus' appearance on the "appointed" mountain in Galilee took place sometime after His shoreline appearance. We don't know what mountain the disciples were directed to. Was it the same mountain where He fed the five thousand? Was it the same mountain where He prayed before walking toward them upon the water? We tend to think of it as the same mountain on which He was tempted during His own commissioning for ministry and mission.

Most likely this mountain meeting is when Jesus appeared to more than five hundred people at once (1 Cor. 15:6). The fact that Matthew distinguishes the disciples who "worshiped" Him from others who "doubted" suggests the presence of many followers who had not known Jesus well before, much less spoken or eaten with Him. The Greek word *distazo*, which we translate as "doubting," really means "wavering," or "vacillating," such as the hesitancy of Peter when he realized he was walking on the water and the wind was kicking up. Even "mountain men" hesitate.

God speaks loudest on mountains.

Think Mount Moriah, Mount Sinai, Mount Zion, Mount Carmel, Sermon on the Mount, Mount Calvary. Eden itself is seen as a mountain garden, with rivers flowing downhill. It was here that God walked and talked with us in the dew of day, telling us, "You are chosen and cherished. I delight in your presence." The first altars were mini-mountains erected for worship in garden groves with wells—worship where hearing God's voice makes our hearts sing and minds dance.

> *Great things are done when men and mountains meet.*
>
> —WILLIAM BLAKE[1]

Whether we hear His mountain voice or His valley voice, the question is whether we can hear God speak. The Midrash teaches that at the time of the greatest show on earth, the crossing of the sea on dry ground, there were those who missed the moment. "The sea floor was covered, as one would expect, with mud, still moist from the ocean water. Whereupon one 'Reuben' remarked to one 'Simeon,' 'What's the difference?! In Egypt we had mud. Here we have mud.'"[2]

Can God say anything to someone not ready to hear it? If we had been at Sinai, would we have heard it? If we had been on any of those mountaintops when Jesus spoke the loudest, would we have had ears to hear? Or would we only have seen the mud?

Jesus loved to escape to the mountains almost as much as He loved the sea. "When Jesus saw the crowds, He went up on the mountain; and after He sat down, His disciples came to Him" (Matt. 5:1 NASB). What happened next after the disciples left the crowd and got close to Jesus? They were blessed with eight beatitudes. Want to hear Jesus? Want to be blessed? Leave the crowd. Look up and listen up. Come close to Jesus. Incline your hearing to the Lord, so that you can incline your hearts to the Lord.

Discipleship is an acoustical art. In ancient Sumerian, the words for *ear* and *wisdom* are the same. Turn your head and tune your ears to the mountain:

I will lift up mine eyes unto the hills, from whence cometh my help. (Ps. 121:1 KJV)

"And I, if I am lifted up from the earth, will draw all men to Myself." (John 12:32 NASB)

"Lift up your hearts!"
"We lift them up to the Lord!"[3]

No matter how weary, weighed down, and wounded your heart, it is not too heavy to lift to the Lord. The mountains "lift up" our souls in three ways: First, the mountains echo the distant songs of a lost paradise. Second, the mountains megaphone the Scriptures so that they speak for themselves and echo without distortion and delusion. Third, the mountains expose those who don't want to hear God but just want to hear their own echoes.

The veil of glory, momentarily pulled back on the mountain of the transfiguration, is torn in two from top to bottom by the cross of Mount Calvary, the last mountain to climb. The light of God's ineffable love for us shines out from that mount; the light that Moses, Elijah, and Abraham began to see, but only from their vantage point on the top of the mountain. The mountaintop revelation to a chosen few has become the sign lifted up from the earth for all men to see and be drawn to. As Jesus taught from another mountain by Galilee: "Do not think that I have come to abolish the Law or the Prophets; I have not come to abolish them but to fulfill them" (Matt. 5:17).

So in order to best hear Jesus speak, we pilgrimage to the "mountain." We make pilgrimages to holy places, because that's where our hearing is most acute. Martin Luther and some of the Reformers pooh-poohed any religious significance to the Holy Land and to the whole concept of holy places, saying "As for the tomb in which the Lord lay, which the Saracens now possess, God values it like all the cows in Switzerland."[4] But holy places have meaning, and each of us may have a different holy place.

We all must hear God's voice when going through a valley. But you can't have a valley without two mountains, and God leads us through the valley to the mountains. In Psalm 22, there is a mountain: Calvary, where Jesus was crucified and died, the culmination of His first coming. In Psalm 23, there is a valley: the Valley of the Shadow, even Sheol itself, where we look for the light as we navigate and negotiate the shadows, even the "valley of the shadow of death" (v. 4 KJV). In Psalm 24, there is a mountain: resurrection morning, a world-changing historical event with world-shaking significance.

> *Doubt is an act in which the mind inspects its own ideals; wonder is an act in which the mind confronts the universe.*
>
> —RABBI ABRAHAM HESCHEL[5]

If you had to choose a place, a landscape, that best explained who you are, what would you pick? We suspect Jesus would have picked the mountains. Jesus goes to the mountain to pray throughout His ministry, and for Jesus to "teach us to pray" (Luke 11:1) is to "teach us to live" (Ps. 90:12, author's paraphrase). He spends His last moment with His disciples on the mountain.

On this mountain, a new covenant is passed on to the disciples. In the first covenant, we were told to "be fruitful and multiply" (Gen. 1:22 NKJV). In this new covenant, we are told to do the same—missionize ("be fruitful") and baptize ("multiply"). On this mountain, disciples became disciplers; acolytes became apostles; men became "mountain men."

If the church had only listened better to Jesus, it wouldn't have wasted millions of hours concocting "mission statements." The church has a mission statement already, provided directly by Jesus: "Go into the world and make disciples of all cultures" and proclaim Christ's mission! Christ's mission is not a statement, however, but an endowment and an engagement. It's a mission that can be derided, delayed, and detoured, but not defeated.

> "The Spirit of the Lord is upon me,
>> because he has anointed me
>> to proclaim good news to the poor.
> He has sent me to proclaim liberty to the captives
>> and recovering of sight to the blind,
>> to set at liberty those who are oppressed,
> to proclaim the year of the Lord's favor." (Luke 4:18–19 ESV)

A God-hearer will be a mission-bearer.

God gave Ezekiel a vision of the temple now restored, saying, "This is the place of my throne . . . where I will dwell in the midst of the people of Israel forever" (Ezek. 43:7 ESV). The gospel says that in Jesus, God is dwelling with us. When the Gospels talk to us about Jesus, they are saying to us: Remember Abraham on that starry night? Remember Moses and the burning bush? Remember Jeremiah's yoke worn around his neck? Remember Moses' wilderness tabernacle and the altar of incense? Remember Solomon's temple on Mount Zion and the ark of the covenant?

"Take heed how you hear."

—JESUS (LUKE 8:18 NKJV)

To "go"—or better yet, "to be in a state of going"—is the art of mission. To "make disciples" is the art of relationship, which is more than checking off converts. To plant Jesus "in all cultures" is the mark of incarnation.

First, the art of mission. There is a lot of missional malarky out there, but fundamentally, Jesus is commissioning us all as missionaries, who are being sent into the mission field. John Calvin defined a faithful disciple as someone busy on mission, in motion, but with a still and reposed mind.[6]

You hear Jesus best "as you are going," in the motion of mission. Listening to the Bible speak to itself is not God's mission. Listening to the Bible speak to the world is God's mission. Nothing blocks the voice of Jesus like living between the dead-ends of book-ends. Nothing sets free Jesus' voice like taking that book on an ends-of-the-earth mission.

The missional life is not a glamorous life. We would like Jesus to make us (His disciples) lords of our little kingdoms, but Jesus instead knights the benighted and sends us out to anoint those who have nothing and can do nothing for us. Jesus washes the feet of the servants; God chooses a servant girl to exalt among women. Never did someone cry out for help but that Jesus stopped to listen. The aphorism "you don't get to choose your family" is true. Even the genealogy of Jesus (Matt. 1:1–17) had enough scandals to keep tabloids busy for years. Except it seems that Jesus purposely chose and chooses the weak and the flawed, the failed and the flailing, to shine and showcase God's greatness.

You are hearing Jesus when you hear the heartbreak. The true treasury of the church is not filled with stocks but stories, not wealthy people being heralded but wounded people being helped and healed. Do you find yourself always buying presents for the person who has everything? Maybe it's time to expand your circle of friends to include the person who has nothing. Listen to Jesus:

> "'I was a stranger, and you did not invite Me in; naked, and you did not clothe Me; sick, and in prison, and you did not visit Me.' Then they themselves also will answer, 'Lord, when did we see You hungry, or thirsty, or a stranger, or naked, or sick, or in prison, and did not take care of You?' Then He will answer them, 'Truly I say to you, to the extent that you did not do it to one of the least of these, you did not do it to Me.'" (Matt. 25:43–45 NASB)

Second, the ark of relationship. A vibrant, vital relationship with Christ is at the heart of knowing God and hearing God speak.

What made the Holy of Holies so holy was not the ark, or the art, or the timeless truths engraved in stone or abstracted in doctrines. What made the Holy of Holies so holy was the presence of the living God in the mercy seat. The holy is participation in the presence of the divine. Jesus didn't leave us with an ethic. He left us with an ethos—a missional, relational, incarnational ethos—for the living of these days; not a program or a platform or a principle, but a presence and a power.

"It is required in a good servant, to have the back of an Asse, to bear all things patiently, the tongue of a sheepe, to keep silence gently; and the snout of a swine, to feede on all things heartily."

—LEONARD WRIGHT, *A DISPLAY OF DUTIE, DECT WITH SAGE SAYINGS, PYTHIE SENTENCES, AND PROPER SIMILIES* (1589)

All of us have a "secret place," a Holy of Holies within the heart where an ark is hidden. Does Jesus alone, the heart of heaven, have the keys to our hearts? There are many dead ways of life, but Jesus is the Living Way. Life is not to be like Jesus; Jesus *is* life. Imagine what could happen if we began to receive Christ's commission as a relational consciousness of the living Christ.

Jesus didn't drop off a scroll of rules on the mountain; He appeared to followers. The core of faith is not cognition, but recognition. God is not like us; we are like God (Gen. 1:27). And since we are people, we can conclude God is a person. Because we exist for love, for loving relationships, we can conclude that God is love and is in love with all of us. So we can address God relationally, as "Abba," not as some "Great Ground of Being" or "First Principle" or "Immortal Lawgiver."

Third, the mark of incarnation. A young missionary came to a tribe in Namibia. After preaching the gospel and telling them about Jesus, how He lived and what He did, the Namibians stopped him and told him, "We know this man you are talking about, for He lived with us!"

Confused (because his mission agency told him he was the first to witness to this tribe), he asked, "When did he live here?"

"Five years ago," they replied.

"That couldn't be," the missionary said. "The man I am talking about, Jesus of Nazareth, has been dead for two thousand years."

"No, no," they protested. "He lived among us, and became one of us. He spoke like us, and even came to look like us. And we'll prove it to you."

So they took him to a grave, where they showed him the tombstone and pointed to his name. It was the only name they knew him by: "Reverend." The epitaph on the tombstone read: *Reverend: 1897–1963.*

Then the missionary understood. The gospel he was preaching, the message he was trying to tell them . . . this missionary named "Reverend" . . . was the way he lived among them. It was a gospel without words. After various discussions he found out that the night before "Reverend" died, all the villagers came to say good-bye. One elderly woman, whose English wasn't that good, told the missionary what she said to the dying man: "Reverend, I like me the best when I'm with you! Thank you for coming to live with us. Thank you for your life."

Jesus Speaks . . . in His Trinitarian Voice

As Jesus prepared to ascend to heaven, He revealed the name of God to His disciples. This arrived as another startling revelation. Till that time, the Israelites considered God's "name"—His innermost identity—unutterable. Yet Jesus spoke it as something intimate, a family name: "the name of the Father and of the Son and of the Holy Spirit" (Matt. 28:19).

No one thought to correct our Lord, pointing out that there seemed to be *three* names in His statement, though He used the singular word *name.* In this line, as in that first chapter of Genesis,[7] there appears to be a paradox: a plurality yet a unity. We speak of name, not "names." Because God is one, there is only one God—Father-Son-Holy Spirit.

The Alone One, beside which there is none other (Isa. 45:5), is not alone but exists in triune community. Nothing significant exists outside of relationship. When Jesus revealed God's name, Jesus revealed God as a family: Father, Son, and Holy Spirit, a divine *we* in relational terms, not biological terms or gender terms.

It is important for us to hear God as Father, Son, and Holy Spirit, and not some other language. When we refer to God as Father, Son, and Holy Spirit, we refer to *who God is*. When we refer to God as Creator, Redeemer, Sanctifier, we refer to God in terms of *what God has done.* Do you love your spouse because of what he or she has done for you, or because of who he or she is?

The Trinity is a Love Triangle: the Lover (the Father), the Loved (the Son), and the Love (the Holy Spirit) who unites Lover and Loved. The triangulated path of discipleship is the increasing ability to hear the three-way dialogue that moves along all sides of the Love Triangle.

Jesus' Final Meetings

Jesus met with His half brother James after appearing on the mountain (1 Cor. 15:7). While we cannot be sure of the place of this meeting, it makes sense that it would have happened in Galilee, since that is where Jesus and James grew up, and where James shows up in the gospel narratives (Matt. 12:46–50; cf. Matt. 13:55). Wherever this meeting occurred, it seems to have been a catalyst for James, who was a skeptic (John 7:5), to believe that his half brother truly was and is the Son of God. James went on to write what some scholars say is the earliest written book of the Bible.

Paul also explained that Christ was seen by all the apostles one more time after His visit with James (1 Cor. 15:7). This event is recorded in

Acts 1 (cf. Matt. 28:18–20; Mark 16:14–19; Luke 24:44–53). Jesus led the apostles as far as Bethany, on the eastern side of Mount Olivet, near Jerusalem. There He gave them their final instructions before He ascended into heaven.

For the practical application of the themes mentioned
in this chapter, see chapter 43 in volume 2.

EIGHT

The Godstruck Voice of Jesus

Jesus' Eighth Appearance: Jesus Speaks Through the Holy Spirit at Pentecost

---

Look down and see this waiting host,
Give us the promised Holy Ghost,
We want another Pentecost,
Send the fire!

—WILLIAM BOOTH, COFOUNDER
OF THE SALVATION ARMY[1]

"Going Is Coming": Pentecost

As has already been discussed in previous chapters, Jesus told His disciples not to leave Jerusalem, but to wait for the promise of the Father, who would baptize them in the Holy Spirit. He told them that it was not for them to know the times and dates that the Father has set by His own authority and that they would receive power when the Holy Spirit came upon them, making them His witnesses from Jerusalem to the ends of the earth (Acts 1:4–8).

Transitions are never easy, for the child or the parent. Our relationship with God is the ultimate parent-child relationship, and transitions are not easy for our divine Parent either. As Eve undoubtedly said to Adam as they were being ushered out of the walk-and-talk intimacy of the garden, "We are living in a time of great transition."[2] In the fall, we experienced the first Great Transition in history. Jesus, the Second Adam, would usher in the second.

Jesus Speaks . . . in His Future Voice

"But I tell you the truth; it is better for you that I go away, for if I may not go away, the Comforter will not come unto you, and if I go on, I will send Him unto you."

—JOHN 16:7 YLT

Jesus said to His disciples, "It is better for you that I go away." How could it be "better" that the Savior of the world, the very Son of God, "go away"? Why would Jesus make such a statement?

Simple. Because Jesus, who had been *with* them, was going to be *inside* of them by the power of the Holy Spirit!

Jesus had a succession plan unlike one anyone has ever conceived in history, a succession where Jesus would be more physically present in death than in life. How could this possibly be? His successors would be every one of us, a potential activated by the Spirit into a presence and a power. This succession would not be mere role-playing Jesus. It would be Jesus.

Jesus declared that He would be gone, and yet He would always be present. Though His declaration was made to His first disciples, it was also a promise to all of His disciples who were to come.

How devastating must this news have been to Jesus' original disciples. The disciples' problem is our problem: their understanding of "change" was limited to a human lifetime horizon. The divine vision, the divine horizon, however, is a much more expansive and embracing one.

Jesus chided His first followers for not asking Him about the future, for not asking the right questions. Part of hearing Jesus speak is getting a future frame of mind, which leads to the right kinds of asking.

"But now the time has come for me to go away to the one who sent me. None of you asks me, 'Where are you going?'" (John 16:5–6 PHILLIPS)

Here is a "tell" that reveals a "tale" to Jesus of how far His first disciples were from having a "forward focus" on His mission. The disciples heard Jesus' predictions of arrest, crucifixion, death, and resurrection. All of His predictions had come true. What had been foretold had passed, but the future still stretched out in front of them. Their perspectives were so time-bound and earth-bordered that they could not comprehend the whole picture Jesus was revealing to them. The best had yet to come. They needed pentecost to "get it." The first generation of disciples kept asking "Why?" and failing to ask "Where?" and "Who?"

Jesus is always present yet absent. It sounds a bit loopy, but this is the way, truth, and life. We don't leap forward; we loop forward. Our movement is not linear but loopy. In fact, if you combine the line and the circle, you get a loop, or in 3-D, a spiral. We reach forward to the future by a going-back motion that incorporates the past before the loop of the spiral thrusts forward. The past is not left behind. The past is reconceived and re-appropriated afresh whenever a new loop is realized. All tenses of time (past, present, future) are folded into Jesus, the fulfillment of history.

Why is it good for us that Jesus goes away? Why might it be easier for us to hear Jesus speaking if He has gone away than if He were physically present?

Jesus Speaks . . . in His Pentecost Voice

First, His going away enables the coming of the Spirit. Something more miraculous and long lasting was on its way. In an amazing passage,

Jesus called John the Baptist the greatest prophet in history. Then He added that every single follower is now greater than John. Jesus put the cherry on top in this stunning claim: "Whoever is least in the kingdom of heaven is greater than [John]" (Matt. 11:11).

What could Jesus have meant? How could the "least" of us be more privileged and blessed than the "greatest" prophet in history?

First, we know the full story of Jesus better than John ever did. John was beheaded before Jesus' story unfolded and fulfilled the Scriptures. Even though we, too, are in a world that wants to take our heads off, we are still better off than John, since we know the plot of this never-ending story.

Second, Jesus said it was good that He was going away. Admittedly, it was a tough sell.

But Jesus' going away released His ongoing incarnation through the power of the Holy Spirit. The release of the divine into the human is made available to all human beings through the power of the Holy Spirit to bring Christ to life in each one of us. "Emmanuel" or "God-with-us" means more than a one-shot appearance. Jesus never wanted to be born solely into first-century Palestine. Jesus wants to be born into and heard speaking out of the hearts and minds of all human beings.

That is why we have pentecost. The Holy Spirit is God's breath. God's voice is made audible by the Spirit. Without breath, you can hear no words. The breath brings the words into speech. When you're out of breath, you can barely talk.

Jesus announced His leaving to His first-century disciples so He could speak to all generations of disciples, so He could be there for all. The sword of the Spirit plows into the ground of every soul as the voice of Jesus. The Spirit wants to be the Voice heard so deeply that you yourself become that voice.

The first generation of disciples didn't get it until after pentecost. The pentecost moment keeps recurring with the confession of every new disciple. The Holy Spirit keeps Jesus alive and speaking in us today. That's why it's important to "keep pentecost."[3] It's the way we become and grow as "little Christs," the literal meaning of *Christ-ians*. It's the way we hear Jesus speaking.

Jesus wants to be born again in each one of us. The pentecost gift of the Holy Spirit is the gift of the ongoing incarnation of Jesus among all His disciples, always and forever. At pentecost we sing "Happy Birthday" to the church. But the church is called "the body of Christ" for a reason. Pentecost, the gift of the Holy Spirit, is the only reason there is a community of disciples, a body of faith, that continues to be connected to Christ.

Jesus Speaks ... in His Holy Spirit Voice

This is going to seem strange to read in a Jesus book, but it needs to be said: we can overemphasize Jesus. If we fail to live trinitarily, if we put the third person of the Trinity in third place rather than a coequal place with the Father and Son, we are neglecting the Holy Spirit. And to neglect the Spirit is to neglect Christ, for Jesus Himself said, "It is better for you that I go away, for I will send you the Spirit, who will guide you into all truth" (John 16:7, authors' paraphrase).

The Holy Spirit brings Jesus' voice to life though history, theology, science,[4] and social experience. Jesus told the disciples, "I have much more to say to you" (John 16:12). In other words, Jesus was saying, "You can't handle everything I have to say to you right now. Some of My truth has a wavelength, and it needs time, maybe even centuries, to play itself out." Sometimes Jesus says things to us and gives us thoughts that are so true we do not comprehend them, or more accurately, we are not in a place to understand what Jesus is saying. We can trust the Holy Spirit to lead us "into all the truth" (John 16:13) as a quarterback leads a receiver. We just have to keep running and stay faithful to the "play" of the Spirit. Jesus didn't give anyone the whole truth all at once.

The Holy Spirit that leads us into all truth is the Spirit of Christ. There is no more truth than is found in Christ. Christ is the all in all, all God has to teach us. All the treasures of wisdom and knowledge are hidden in Him (Col. 2:3). There is no higher revelation, no higher truth, than Jesus. But the fact that God has no more to teach us than Jesus, the fact that there is no more to learn than is found in Christ, does *not* mean that we do not have a great deal more to learn or that God does not have anything more to teach us. The riches and wisdom of Christ are inexhaustible. God has no more to give us than has been given in Jesus, but we have a great deal more to receive—hence we enjoy a lifelong feast on Him in our hearts with thanksgiving.

When you hear the Spirit, you are hearing the Son. If it doesn't sound like the Son, it's not the Spirit. The Son and Spirit are a tag-team match, always speaking and acting in tandem with each other. The members of the Trinity are not in competition with each other, but what the Son can do, the Spirit can do even better. It is only because of who the Spirit is and what the Spirit does that the Son is who He is and is able to do what He does.

Jesus' going away enables the ongoing incarnation. God's self-giving love issues in the creation of incarnation. That continuing creation of incarnation makes each of us a Virgin Mary: we are to give virgin birth to the Son, to be mothers of God in our person and in our place. That's why we can never lose the language of "born again." Jesus wants to be born again in us and in our community, and we are called to be born from above by His Spirit.

> *For the Word of God and God wills always and in all things to accomplish the mystery of His embodiment.*
>
> —MAXIMUS THE CONFESSOR (580–662)[5]

Jesus put His disciples in the incarnation and epiphany business. In fact, the Christian faith is an embodied experience of incarnation. Any attempt to make it into a religion of explanation, examination, or execution is an abomination.

God the Potter creates with two hands: Word and Spirit. The three are distinct but inseparable. Both Word and Spirit are present before, during, and after the coming of the Incarnate Word and Pentecostal

Spirit, and both always reference each other. You can't have one without the other.

We translate *Logos* as "Word": "In the beginning was the Word, and the Word was with God, and the Word *was* God" (John 1:1). But God doesn't think in words. God's original word for "dirt" is the dirt. God's original word for "flower" is the flower. God's original word for "water" is the water. God's original word for "wind" is the wind. God's original word for "Truth" is Jesus.

God speaks the language of incarnation. If we want to talk about the deepest things of life, we must break through the language barrier and enter the world of art, music, festival, and dance. In fact, scientists are learning that words come last when it comes to how our brains process information. Your brain first thinks in metaphor, then in narrative, last in words. (When you dream, do you dream in words?) Since there are no words outside of languages, if God spoke in words, what language does God speak? God speaks the language of love, the language of incarnation each of us hears best.

There was only one physical incarnation. But there is a pentecostal incarnation ("until Christ be formed in you," Gal. 4:19 KJV) for each person who invites Jesus into his or her life.

The physical incarnation gave the first generation of disciples the gift of a Jesus alongside them. The pentecostal incarnation gives all future disciples the gift of a Jesus within and among us.

Losing the physical incarnation of Jesus was an immense personal casualty. But gaining the pentecostal incarnation of the ongoing presence of Jesus is an immeasurable triumph. Jesus' testimony "it is better for you that I go away" meant that losing His physical presence became an avenue to gaining His ongoing presence. Of course, until pentecost, no one understood that. After the gift of the Holy Spirit at pentecost, everything became clear, and Jesus now became not physically clear but crystal clear. He made His presence crystalline—to those who believed.

John Bell of the Iona Abbey in Scotland wrote:

Light looked down and saw the darkness.

"I will go there," said light.

Peace looked down and saw war.

"I will go there," said peace.

Love looked down and saw hatred.

"I will go there," said love.

So he,

the Lord of Light,

the Prince of Peace,

the King of Love,

came down and crept in beside us.[6]

Jesus Speaks . . . in His Mysterious Voice

The ears come alive with the soul when Jesus moves in and lives in us. Incarnation is not incarceration but habitation.

But incarnation cuts both ways: what Jesus says will have greater meaning but also greater mystery. Just because Jesus is the perfect revelation of God doesn't mean that anyone knows that revelation perfectly. Part of Jesus speaking leans toward greater accessibility and clarity. But Jesus speaks in a dialect of heaven, a foreign accent that this fallen world and our feeble ears will never get exactly right at first or understand easily and completely.

One way you know you're hearing Jesus speak is if a part of it leaves you with incomprehension and even contradiction, such as what Simeon shared with Mary in the temple concerning her infant son: "He is destined to be a sign which men reject; many in Israel will stand or fall because of him" (Luke 2:34, author's paraphrase). Until the physical return of Jesus, we must have an angular relationship with the world. Jesus' voice communicates and conceals at the same time. Some things are so confusing and complicated that the best we can do is just stop trying to juggle the complexities, throw all the balls up in the air, and tell the Holy Spirit, "You sort it out."

The summit of human fulfillment is not to be a leader, or CEO, or celebrity, but to be a follower of Jesus and manifest Christ in whatever it is you are doing. By the way, the Greek word for "manifest" (*phanerósis*) means to literally throb with a physical appearing.

Jesus Speaks . . . in His Embodied Voice

Jesus' going away directs our ears away from His physical body and toward the corporate body. Jesus' personal voice is inseparable from His physical body, the church. The body of Christ is the preferred canvas over which the Spirit speaks and on which the Spirit draws the destiny of God's dreams and writes the story of God's love for the world.

Jesus weans His disciples from His physical body like this: "In a little while you will see me no more, and then after a little while you will see me" (John 16:16). Or as He told Mary in His first postresurrection appearance: "Do not cling to Me" (John 20:17 NKJV). We cannot cling to Jesus' physical presence. We must focus our hearing not on His corporal body, but on His corporate body.

Christ is the place of God, and the church is the place of Christ. God can be heard without Christ, but only faintly and imperfectly. You can hear Christ outside the church, but with the same proviso. The temple of the Holy Spirit is not the individual. The temple of the Holy Spirit is the body of Christ, which is composed of individuals sharing life together in community.

The Spirit and the church are one. From the middle of the second century, there arose an early baptismal creed that concludes with these words: "I believe in the Holy Spirit, and the church." You can't separate the Spirit and the church; when you get one, you get the other. You can't be a follower of Jesus without being part of a community. The Story has continued to be interpreted and incarnated in the life of the community of faith called the church, a phenomenon called the *sensus fidelium*, or the sense of the faithful.

Hearing Jesus speak involves this table-community "church." It is both communal and personal. Church might even be called a Universal-Particular, as expressed in "Now you are the body of Christ [Universal], and each one of you is a part of it [Particular]" (1 Cor. 12:27). When the conversation gets so intense and animated at a particular table that it sounds like speaking in tongues, that's the sound of pentecost. When the conversation gets so intense and animated at the church's universal table, that's the sound of pentecost.

The Bread of Life is now the Living Bread, and we must offer that Bread to the world. Otherwise, we are like the Midwestern village that boasts a little shop on the town square. It bears a sign over the door that says "Bake Shop." Inside, you can find chocolate, candy, coffee, comic books, all kinds of pastries, and sweets. No bread.[7]

There are churches like that. The sign of Christ promises food, but inside there is busyness, showbiz, body stimulation galore. But no bread.

As we've mentioned already, the literal meaning of *Christ-ian* is "little Christ." Only "little Christs" can serve that bread. Every person sharing life in community is a "little Christ." Christ's presence now is more profound, and the bread is stronger, than if He were physically present. We will do what He didn't do.

The church is those people who live Jesus. It is not the people who remember Jesus but the people who embody and evidence Jesus' resurrection life.

Jesus Speaks ... in His "Greater Things" Voice

"It is to your advantage that I go away; for if I do not go away, the Helper will not come to you; but if I go, I will send Him to you."
—JOHN 16:7 NASB

One of the most incredible things Jesus ever said to His disciples is: "[You] will do even greater things than these, because I am going to the Father.

And I will do whatever you ask in my name, so that the Father may be glorified in the Son" (John 14:12–13). Did you hear it? Jesus is going away so that we can not only continue His mission on earth, but so that we can do even "greater things" than He did while He was here. Jesus didn't free the slaves. We did. Jesus didn't give women the right to vote. We did. Jesus didn't feed all the hungry in the world. Jesus is expecting us to.

It is only because of who the Spirit is and what the Spirit does that the Son is who He is and is able to do what He does. Therefore it can be concluded that whatever the Son can do, the Spirit can do better.

Jesus wants to live His resurrected life in and through us. The going away of Jesus enables the coming of age of Jesus through the church. It is because of this new, pentecostal incarnation that each new generation of Jesus' disciples are able to fulfill the Jesus commandment that no one wants to talk about: the commandment to "do greater things." This is the essence of what it means to keep pentecost: "do greater things."

Jesus is always saying to us, "Do greater things." What "greater things" will you do this week? The mission of "greater things" is what makes us a Happy Birthday Church. The disciple life is nothing less, nor more, than no-holds-barred, whole-being, "greater-things" participation in the life, death, and resurrection of Jesus.

One of the most theologically sophisticated screenplays ever written is the one for the 2003 film *Bruce Almighty*, written by Steve Koren, Mark O'Keefe, and Steve Oedekerk. When bad things happen in Bruce's life, Bruce blames God and finally declares defiantly that if there is a God, God

---

The Bible ends with the Book of Revelation, "the drawbridge of the Christian citadel let down and the road open once more for the spirit of humanity to travel to the end of time with a renewing and infinitely renewable capacity for fresh religious experience and revelations.

—AFRIKANER NOVELIST/KNIGHT SIR LAURENS VAN DER POST[8]

---

is a bad God. God is bad at being God. In fact, Bruce says he could do God better than God does. So God surprises Bruce and says, "Okay, go ahead. You show me how you could do God better." Here's the conversation:

> **God:** You have all my powers. Use them any way you like. There are just two things you can't do: you can't tell anyone you're God. Believe me, you don't want that kind of attention.
>
> **Bruce:** And the other?
>
> **God:** You can't mess with free will.
>
> **Bruce:** Can I ask why?
>
> **God:** Yes you can! That's the beauty of it.

In the final act, God says to a frustrated and defeated Bruce: "The problem is that people keep looking up, when they should look inside. . . . You want to see a miracle—then be a miracle."[9]

The gift of "greater things" enables each one of us to be a miracle—an ongoing incarnation of the presence of Jesus on earth.

You want to hear Jesus?

Then manifest Jesus. Make this principle your number one relationship rule: *I want to love you as Jesus loves you.*

Jesus Speaks . . . in His Daily Voice

Jesus speaks so we can discover the sacred in our daily life.

We always tilt our ears or look for the divine in the wrong direction: toward someplace else, toward something mysterious and far away, toward something "spiritual." We miss the obvious.

The hardest thing to see or hear is the thing staring you in the face; right in front of your eyes, right within earshot. We try to recapture something that we believe we had years ago in childhood or something that we read about in "spiritual" books. We try to improve our hunting skills so that we can capture an elusive God, a God who does not want to be found.

But God is *not* missing or elusive or invisible. It is *we* who need to make ourselves ready to receive God, who daily knocks at the door of our hearts. In company with the ancient Hebrews, Jesus envisioned no dimensional divide between things physical and spiritual, profane and sacred. One apprehended all of reality by a heightened use of the senses, all of which were "sacred": "Taste and see that the LORD is good" (Ps. 34:8); "Hear, O Israel: The Lord our God, the Lord is one" (Mark 12:29).

Pentecost is not just about signs and wonders, but about experiencing the holy in the hubbub and humdrum of the everyday.

Holy is to be found in what appears to be the ordinary, but in truth, there is no ordinary.

Creation itself is a divine signpost that speaks of Jesus to listening ears: "All nature sings, and round me rings the music of the spheres."[10] "The heavens declare the glory of God," and "the glory of God in the face of Jesus Christ" (Ps. 19:1; 2 Cor. 4:6 ESV). Everything that exists bears the imprint of its Creator. In fact, it is kept in existence by that divine breath. May God help us hear into dance the mystery of wholeness and the beauty of holiness.

Hearing the Voice That Has No Words

PART ONE

Tuning Your Ears to Hear

NINE

Become Poor in Spirit

Becoming poor in spirit is the first requirement for recognizing the voice of Jesus.

What does it mean to be poor in spirit?

The Pharisees were rich in spirit.

The scribes were rich in spirit.

And so were the Christians in Laodicea: "You say, 'I am rich; I have acquired wealth and do not need a thing.' But you do not realize that you are wretched, pitiful, poor, blind and naked" (Rev. 3:17).

On the other hand, the publicans (tax collectors) were poor in spirit.

The prostitutes were poor in spirit.

The poor and oppressed were poor in spirit.

Jesus drove a standard in the ground when He said that the kingdom of the heavens (the unseen, heavenly realm where Christ rules) belongs to the poor in spirit. Hearing the voice of Jesus is part of that other realm.

Being poor in spirit, then, means having a childlike humility and a poverty-stricken desperation for the Lord.

Jesus Himself showed us what being poor in spirit was all about. He who was rich emptied Himself and became a slave "taking the form of a bond-servant" (Phil. 2:7 NASB).

Each day that He lived on this earth, Jesus lived in constant desperation and neediness for His Father. He indicated this when He said, "I can do nothing on my own" (John 5:30 NLT).

Then He turned around and said to you, "Apart from me you can do nothing" (John 15:5).

Do you want to hear the Lord speak and keep speaking?

Become poor in spirit. And stay poor in spirit.

No matter how much the Lord shows you and does through you, it's vital that you remain desperate for Him.

Why? Because the day you stop being desperate and needy for your Lord is the day when you will have become rich in spirit.

And this will mute your ears to the voice of Christ.

"Blessed are the poor in spirit, for theirs is the kingdom of heaven." (Matthew 5:3)

TEN

Reject Condemnation

One of the greatest hindrances to hearing the voice of the Lord is our sense of guilt, condemnation, and unworthiness. Such feelings are all too common among Christians today, even though Jesus has set us free from each of them.

When Christians feel that God doesn't like them, that He's upset with them, or that they aren't "spiritual" enough to hear Jesus speak to them, they close their spiritual ears to His voice without realizing it.

The antidote for a clear conscience is the blood of Christ. It is through the blood that you stand in the perfect righteousness of Jesus Himself. And it is through trusting in that blood that your conscience becomes clear.

The good news of the gospel is that you can do nothing to make yourself more acceptable to God over and above what Jesus has already done at Calvary. You cannot add to it, and you cannot take away from it. Consequently, we are never to approach God on the basis of our own works, but solely on the work of Another.

Nothing can arm a Christian with pure conscience except for the blood of Christ.

By trusting in the blood, the sense of unworthiness, the sense of guilt, and the sense of condemnation are removed.

How much more, then, will the blood of Christ, who through the eternal Spirit offered himself unblemished to God, cleanse our consciences from acts that lead to death, so that we may serve the living God! (Heb. 9:14)

Your acceptance before God is not a question of your efforts, how well you did this week, how much you read the Bible or prayed or resisted temptation. Your acceptance is always a question of what Jesus Christ has done for you. It is through His shed blood that you have made your peace with God.

Again, your acceptance before God must always and forever be based on Christ's work. That work is a final and finished work. And it was enough to satisfy the holy demands of a just God.

Take note: Jesus' shed blood always looms larger in God's eyes than your fallen state. Thus when we believe our feelings of unworthiness, guilt, and condemnation above what God's Word has said about the power of the blood, we make God out to be a liar.

If we confess our sins, he is faithful and just and will forgive us our sins and purify us from all unrighteousness. (1 John 1:9)

When you repented and trusted in Jesus as Lord and Savior, you were granted perpetual access to the throne of God because of the shed blood of Christ on your behalf.

The veil in the temple that separated God's holy presence from fallen humanity was torn in two by the death of Jesus (Luke 23:45), giving you immediate access to the Lord:

Therefore, brothers and sisters, since we have confidence to enter the Most Holy Place by the blood of Jesus, by a new and living way opened for us through the curtain, that is, his body, and since we have a great priest over the house of God, let us draw near to God with a sincere heart and with the full assurance that faith brings, having our hearts sprinkled to cleanse us from a guilty conscience and having our bodies washed with pure water. (Heb. 10:19–22)

Let us then approach God's throne of grace with confidence, so that we may receive mercy and find grace to help us in our time of need. (Heb. 4:16)

You may say in your heart, "But I'm not worthy to hear the voice of Jesus."

Yes, you are not worthy—in yourself. But the beauty of the gospel is that you are not in yourself. *You are in Christ!*

The Lord Jesus Christ, then, is our acceptance, and God has placed you in Him.

Once you were alienated from God and were enemies in your minds because of your evil behavior. But now he has reconciled you by Christ's physical body through death to present you holy in his sight, without blemish and free from accusation. (Col. 1:21–22)

Satan's chief tack is to unseat your righteous place in Christ. It's to inflict you with guilt and condemnation, causing you to question your acceptance and your right standing with God.

The enemy's most powerful weapon is accusation. And the remedy for it is to arm yourself with a clean conscience through the blood of Christ.

> "For the accuser of our brothers and sisters,
>   who accuses them before our God day and night,
>   has been hurled down.
> They triumphed over him
>   by the blood of the Lamb
>   and by the word of their testimony;
> they did not love their lives so much
>   as to shrink from death." (Rev. 12:10–11)

Believe and accept the value of the blood of Christ as God sees it. Believe that it completely satisfies His requirements, because it does.

This is the only way to be freed from a sense of guilt, condemnation, and unworthiness—removing all blockages to hearing His voice.

ELEVEN

Always Remain a Child

If you believe that your opinions are superior to those of others, that you are smarter and more spiritual, then you will have difficulty recognizing Jesus when He speaks to you.

Consider Isaiah 28:9:

> "To whom will he teach knowledge,
>   and to whom will he explain the message?
> Those who are weaned from the milk,
>   those taken from the breast?" (ESV)

The rest of this text predicts the coming of the Holy Spirit.

Isaiah asked, who does the Lord teach knowledge? His answer: the babes. In other words, those who are humble and dependent, like infants.

Jesus echoed Isaiah, saying, "I praise you, Father, Lord of heaven and earth, because you have hidden these things from the wise and learned, and revealed them to little children" (Matt. 11:25).

The Corinthian church was splitting because of strife and contentions. Proverbs tells us that "where there is strife, there is pride, but wisdom is found in those who take advice" (Prov. 13:10).

The Corinthians were full of pride. For this reason, Paul said that they weren't able to receive the things of the Spirit: "But people who aren't spiritual can't receive these truths from God's Spirit. It all sounds foolish to them and they can't understand it, for only those who are spiritual can understand what the Spirit means. Those who are spiritual can evaluate all things, but they themselves cannot be evaluated by others" (1 Cor. 2:14–15 NLT).

The person who is natural (without the Spirit) doesn't recognize the things of God. Yet the person who is spiritual (the one who is walking in the Spirit) discerns or evaluates all things.

The Corinthian Christians weren't able to recognize the Lord's voice, because they were walking in their flesh. As Paul put it: "But I, brothers, could not address you as spiritual people, but as people of the flesh, as infants in Christ. I fed you with milk, not solid food, for you were not ready for it. And even now you are not yet ready, for you are still of the flesh" (1 Cor. 3:1–3 ESV). So the problem in Corinth was arrogance, which produced jealousy, conflicts, and division (1 Cor. 1–3).

By contrast, childlike humility and a reverential awe of the Lord is what attunes our ears to hear the voice of the Savior.[1]

> The secret of the LORD is for those who fear Him,
> And He will make them know His covenant. (Ps. 25:14 NASB)

A great illustration of this principle is Moses. He was close to God because he was more humble than his peers (Num. 12:3).

Do you want to recognize the voice of Jesus?

Become like a little child, and remain one.

> He guides the humble in what is right
> and teaches them his way. (Ps. 25:9)

TWELVE

Exercise Faith

The Bible is clear that faith allows us to receive from God. Both salvation and sanctification (walking in holiness) are obtained by faith.

The same is true with hearing the Lord's voice. We often don't hear the Lord speaking to us because we don't expect Him to.

Let's first be clear on this: the idea that God doesn't speak to His children anymore (except when they read the Bible) is false. There is nothing in Scripture to indicate that God stopped speaking to His people or that His voice has been replaced by the completion of the Bible or the birth of the church.

Christians aren't to be biblical deists, people who believe that God no longer communicates directly with His children. They believe He left the Bible for them to figure out what His will is and nothing more.

Jesus had strong words to say to the biblical deists of His day, most of whom knew the Bible extremely well: "And the Father who sent me has himself testified concerning me. You have never heard his voice nor seen his form, nor does his word dwell in you, . . . You study the Scriptures diligently because you think that in them you have eternal life. These are the very Scriptures that testify about me" (John 5:37–39).

Biblical deism is not biblical. God didn't create the world, then leave it on its own, giving us the Bible in place of Himself.

The Scriptures show us the many ways in which God speaks to His children, both past and present. The Bible is but one of them. (More on that later.)

Paul exhorted the Christians in Rome to prophesy according to their faith: "If your gift is prophesying, then prophesy in accordance with your faith" (Rom. 12:6).

Prophecy is speaking what God has revealed. Consequently, hearing God is also according to one's faith.

> Trust in the LORD with all your heart;
>> do not depend on your own understanding.
> Seek his will in all you do,
>> and he will show you which path to take. (Prov. 3:5–6 NLT)

If you don't think God wants to speak to you, then you are living in doubt, and you won't recognize His voice when it comes to you. So the starting point is to believe that God *is* and that "He is a rewarder of those who diligently seek Him" (Heb. 11:6 NKJV).

We prophesy according to our faith. And we recognize the Lord's voice according to our faith. Trust Him to speak to you, and you'll begin to recognize His voice.

As is the case with so many things in the spiritual realm, hearing the voice of Jesus is a matter of exercising faith.

"According to your faith let it be done to you." (Matt. 9:29)

"Let it be done just as you believed it would." (Matt. 8:13)

If any of you lacks wisdom, you should ask God, who gives generously to all without finding fault, and it will be given to you. But when you ask, you must believe and not doubt, because the one who doubts is like a wave of the sea, blown and tossed by the wind. That person should not expect to receive anything from the Lord. Such a person is double-minded and unstable in all they do. (James 1:5–8)

Remember, the Lord has promised that if you are a child of God, you will be led by His Spirit: "Those who are *led* by the Spirit of God are the children of God" (Rom. 8:14).

And hearing is linked to following: "My sheep *hear* My voice, and I know them, and they *follow* Me" (John 10:27 NKJV). We hear Jesus so we can follow Him.

In the next chapter, we'll explore how we can increase our faith to hear the Lord's voice.

For I do not seek to understand in order to believe,
but I believe in order to understand. For I believe
that "Unless I believe, I shall not understand."
—Anselm of Canterbury[1]

THIRTEEN

Increasing Your Faith to Hear

G. Campbell Morgan aptly wrote, "Wherever there are hearts waiting for the voice of God, that voice is to be heard."[1]

The Lord speaks to us in response to our *expectation* that He will speak to us. In other words, we recognize His voice when we believe. But how does one attain such faith?

This question brings us back to the issue of being poor in spirit. Faith operates in the soil of humility. If you are poor in spirit, you've prepared the garden of your heart for faith to grow and flourish.

Do you remember when the disciples once asked Jesus to increase their faith? The Lord's response was to tell them a story about a servant who did all that his master asked. And when the servant was finished serving his master that day, he didn't expect a thank-you or a pat on the back. The servant instead was grateful to have served the master in humility (Luke 17:5–10). The point is that faith increases out of a child-like heart of humble service.

Another important text on this subject is found in John 5, where Jesus asked the Jewish leaders persecuting Him, "How can you believe since you accept glory from one another but do not seek the glory that comes from the only God?" (v. 44).

One of the major obstacles to faith is the hidden desire to receive glory from mere mortals, instead of only caring about the honor that comes from God. You exist to bring honor and glory to the Lord. That's something to always keep in mind. And it's also the secret to having an ever-increasing faith.

> Not to us, Lord, not to us
>> but to your name be the glory,
>> because of your love and faithfulness. (Ps. 115:1)

FOURTEEN

Be Willing to Respond

Another critical ingredient in preparing our spiritual ears to hear the voice of the Lord is a willingness to respond to what He says. Jesus said, "If anyone's will is to do God's will, he will know" (John 7:17 ESV).

If you wish to know the will of God, then you must be willing to *do* His will when it is made known to you. Like humility, the willingness to follow the Lord's voice is a prerequisite to hearing that voice.

> "I judge only as I *hear*, and my judgment is just, for I seek not to please myself but him who sent me." (John 5:30)

> "I do nothing on my own but speak just what the Father has taught me. . . . He has not left me alone, for I always do what pleases him." (John 8:28–29)

Paul exhorted the believers in Rome to offer their bodies as a living sacrifice to God:

> I beseech you therefore, brethren, by the mercies of God, that you present your bodies a living sacrifice, holy, acceptable to God, which is your reasonable service. And do not be conformed to this world, but be

transformed by the renewing of your mind, that you may prove what is that good and acceptable and perfect will of God. (Rom. 12:1–2 NKJV)

Paul went on to discuss the renewing of the mind. The net effect of offering one's body as a living sacrifice and renewing one's mind is the ability to "prove" or demonstrate the perfect will of God.

To put it another way, how often you hear the Lord is directly related to your willingness to act upon what you hear.

"If anyone has ears to hear, let him hear. . . . Take heed what you hear. With the same measure you use, it will be measured to you; and to you who hear, more will be given. For whoever has, to him more will be given; but whoever does not have, even what he has will be taken away from him." (Mark 4:23–25 NKJV)

Paul called himself and his coworkers "bond-servants" of the Lord (Titus 1:1 NASB; 2 Tim. 2:24 NASB; Col. 4:7 NASB). In the Old Testament, a bond servant was one who willingly gave himself in service to his master. To symbolize his devotion, the bond servant's ear was pierced (Ex. 21:5–6). In the same way, bond servants of Jesus Christ must have their ears pierced (spiritually speaking) so they can hear their Master clearly. For what use is a servant if the master doesn't have his ear?

Do you wish to hear the voice of Jesus? Then be willing to obey what He says to you. And do not harden your heart (Heb. 3:15). Else you will neither "hear" nor "understand" when He speaks (Matt. 13:14 NKJV).

"The ox knows its master,
    the donkey its owner's manger,
but Israel does not know,
    my people do not understand." (Isa. 1:3)

"Why do you not understand what I say? It is because you cannot bear to hear my word." (John 8:43 ESV)

Are you having trouble hearing the Lord when you once heard Him before? Then return to the last thing you believe He told you to do, and respond today.

But be doers of the word, and not hearers only, deceiving yourselves. (James 1:22 NKJV)

One further point: because you belong to the Lord, He will never give up on you. So if His children become deaf to His speaking, He will sometimes turn up the volume through their circumstances. This is the principle of loving discipline (Heb. 12:5–9; Rev. 3:19).

But the Lord's chastisement can be avoided if our ears are tuned to His speaking. And this attuning begins with a heart that's willing to respond to His voice.

FIFTEEN

Have the Right Motive

It's all too possible to have the wrong motive when it comes to hearing the Lord's voice.

For instance, if you are only concerned about your own well-being, your future, your success, or any other self-driven intention, you probably won't recognize His voice when it comes to you.

The primary motive for hearing from the Lord is to glorify Him and benefit others. It's not so you can avoid personal problems or get ahead in life. Consequently, the Lord won't cooperate if your intentions are completely self-focused. In such cases, His communication will be blocked.

This issue of focus gets back to God's eternal purpose, which involves conforming you into the image of Christ (Rom. 8:28–30).

You see, the foundation for hearing the Lord to begin with is to understand that the Lord wants you to be shaped by His voice so as to bring Him honor and glory in your life and service.

In Matthew 6:22, Jesus put it this way: "The lamp of the body is the eye. If therefore your eye be in single focus, pure, sound, your whole body will be well lighted" (WUEST). The King James Version, the American Standard Version, the English Revised Version, and the Darby Bible Translation all translate this verse using the word *single* to describe the state of the eye that Jesus has in mind.

If your eye is single in your devotion to the Lord, your whole being will be full of light.

In classical Greek, the word translated *single* in this verse is used figuratively to denote the simplicity of the mind's eye, singleness of purpose, looking straight at its object, as opposed to having two ends in view. This is confirmed by verse 24 when Jesus talks about the problem of having a divided heart: "No one can serve two masters. Either you will hate the one and love the other, or you will be devoted to the one and despise the other."

The same point is made in Proverbs 4:25–27:

> Let your eyes look straight ahead,
> And your eyelids look right before you.
> Ponder the path of your feet,
> And let all your ways be established.
> Do not turn to the right or the left;
> Remove your foot from evil. (NKJV)

According to Jesus, then, a single eye is the key to spiritual enlightenment, while a divided eye brings darkness.

To put it simply, God doesn't exist for your own personal use. To view Him that way is building your life on the wrong foundation.

The purpose of hearing the Lord's voice isn't so you will win in the game of life, or get the upper hand in a debate, or beat someone out of a job.

If we aren't willing to respond to what the Lord reveals to us, then His voice really isn't welcomed in our lives. So ask the Lord to do whatever it takes to align your motives to His in this regard. Thus you will give Him a clear way to speak to you, unhindered.

PART TWO

Hearing Jesus Today

SIXTEEN

What the Forty Days Teach Us

After Jesus rose from the dead, He appeared to His disciples at various times and places over a space of forty days. There are two critical lessons we can learn from this time period that will help us recognize the voice of Jesus today.

A New Way of Hearing

Through His postresurrection appearances, Jesus taught His disciples a new way to know Him. He trained them how to know Him according to the Spirit, rather than according to the flesh (2 Cor. 5:16 NKJV).

After Jesus came out of the grave, His disciples learned to recognize Him, not by His physical appearance, but by His voice. Whenever they saw Him, they didn't recognize Him by His physical appearance. Their recognition was either voice-activated (Luke 24:32; John 20:16) or activated by something He did (Luke 24:30–31).

Jesus made Himself visible to His disciples just enough so they would become used to and confident in His speaking to their spirits. In this way, He was giving them "training wheels" to learn to hear Him without seeing Him, which would happen after He ascended to the Father.

Jesus was teaching His disciples that there would be a new way to "see" Him—not with the physical eye, but with the eyes of the heart.

Today, we serve a Lord who is no longer visible. When Jesus ascended into heavenly realms, He returned in the Spirit—who is invisible. Consequently, Christ is now known, heard, and even "beheld" with spiritual eyes and spiritual ears.

> . . . that the God of our Lord Jesus Christ, the Father of glory, may give to you the spirit of wisdom and revelation in the knowledge of Him, the *eyes* of your understanding being enlightened; that you may know what is the hope of His calling, what are the riches of the glory of His inheritance in the saints. (Eph. 1:17–18 NKJV)

> But we all, with unveiled [open] face, beholding as in a mirror the glory of the Lord, are being transformed into the same image from glory to glory, [even] as by the Spirit of the Lord. (2 Cor. 3:18 NKJV)

> For God, who commanded the light to shine out of darkness, hath shined in our hearts, to give the light of the knowledge of *the glory of God in the face of Jesus Christ.* (2 Cor. 4:6 KJV)

> While we *look not* at the things which are seen, but at the things which *are not seen*; for the things which are seen are temporal, but the things which are not seen are eternal. (2 Cor. 4:18 NASB)

> But *we see Jesus*, who was made a little lower than the angels, for the suffering of death crowned with glory and honor, that He, by the grace of God, might taste death for everyone. (Heb. 2:9 NKJV)

> By faith he [Moses] left Egypt, not being afraid of the anger of the king, for he endured as *seeing him who is invisible.* (Heb. 11:27 ESV)

> *Looking unto Jesus* the author and finisher of our faith; who for the joy

that was set before him endured the cross, despising the shame, and is
set down at the right hand of the throne of God. (Heb. 12:2 KJV)

Jesus said to him, "Have you believed because you have seen me? Blessed
are those who have not seen and yet have believed." (John 20:29 ESV)

> I keep my eyes always on the LORD.
>> With him at my right hand, I will not be shaken. (Ps. 16:8)

As for me, I shall behold your face in righteousness. (Ps. 17:15 ESV)

In God's order of things, the spiritual is supreme over the physical,
the unseen greater than the seen. The infinite is contained within the
invisible; consequently, that which is superior is not visible to the naked
eye (2 Cor. 4:18).

Faith is the gaze of the heart upon the Lord Jesus. It's the lifting up
of our inward eyes to behold Him. In this regard, beholding is believing
(compare John 3:14–15 with Numbers 21:9).

An Elusive Lover

But there is yet another lesson that the forty-day period teaches us.

Jesus Christ is the greatest Lover in the universe. But He's an elusive
Lover. You'll never get to the place in your walk with the Lord where you
have Him figured out, where you can predict His moves, where you can
fully explain Him, box Him in, or hold Him down.

In fact, just when you think you've got ahold of Jesus, He'll slip
through your fingers. He might even appear as a stranger. But upon
second glance, you'll discover that He's no stranger at all. Emmaus will
repeat itself in your life.

Remember Mary Magdalene, the first person to witness the resurrected Christ? When she recognized Him, the first thing she did was
grab Him—and she wouldn't let go.

Jesus responded to her by saying, "Don't cling to me" (John 20:17 NLT).

Why did He say this? Because He had somewhere to go. He was on the move.

Jesus was, in effect, saying to her: "Mary, stop holding on to Me. There's a new way to know Me that's different from what you've experienced thus far. Let Me go, for I must move on. And I want you to follow Me wherever I go."

Jesus is always moving, and the Holy Spirit is beckoning us to "follow the Lamb wherever he goes" (Rev. 14:4). Our tendency is to cling to Him and keep Him where we are.

Like the the maiden who searched for her monarch in the Song of Solomon, our true bridegroom, Jesus, wants us to keep searching for Him.

> My dove in the clefts of the rock,
>> in the hiding places on the mountainside,
> show me your face,
>> let me hear your voice;
> for your voice is sweet,
>> and your face is lovely. (Song 2:14)

> All night long on my bed
>> I looked for the one my heart loves;
>> I looked for him but did not find him.
> I will get up now and go about the city,
>> through its streets and squares;
> I will search for the one my heart loves. (Song 3:1–2)

> Where has your beloved gone,
>> most beautiful of women?
> Which way did your beloved turn,
>> that we may look for him with you? (Song 6:1)

The first problem the disciples had was in recognizing the risen

Christ. And this is still our problem today. Indeed, the Lord wants us to seek Him. He desires that we seek His face (His person), not just His hand (His blessings).

The fact that we must keep seeking Him keeps us humble and hungry. It's the pathway to staying desperate for Him, which is what He desires. Thankfully, He has promised to be found when we seek Him with all our hearts (Jer. 29:13; Matt. 7:7), and His voice will lead us according to His will (Isa. 30:21).

SEVENTEEN

The Lord's Voice in Scripture

We (Frank and Len) both have a high view of the Bible. We believe it's fully inspired, fully authoritative, and fully reliable. And as we made the case in *Jesus: A Theography*, we believe all Scripture, from Genesis to Revelation, tells the story of Jesus Christ.

To be more specific, the Bible reveals a Person who is searching for and reaching out to you, a Person—Jesus—who wants to have an intimate relationship with you. So when we read the Bible, we should read it in a way that helps us search for Christ.

Properly understood, the Bible is God's speech, God's voice, preserved in written form.

The God of creation, embodied in Jesus Christ, spoke directly to the authors of Scripture. And today, He still speaks to His people through both the Old and New Testaments. But the Bible doesn't replace the Lord's personal voice to us.

For instance, the Spirit of Jesus told Philip to walk beside a chariot (Acts 8:29).

He told Peter to go with three men without doubting (Acts 11:12).

The Spirit spoke to Paul, forbidding him to go into certain regions during one of his church-planting trips (Acts 16:6–7).

He told Paul to speak in Corinth and encouraged him not to remain silent (Acts 18:9).

All were cases of specific guidance that couldn't be found in the Bible.

However, the Lord's leading in your life will never contradict the teachings of Scripture. It will *always* be in alignment with them.

Unfortunately, some Christians have used the slogan "The Lord told me . . ." to do things that were clearly sinful and selfish, contradicting the clear teachings of the Bible.

On the other hand, getting immersed in the teachings of Scripture, particularly those of Jesus and the apostles, will help you to better discern the Lord's voice when it comes.

In Scripture, we have a revelation of God's ways, His purpose, and His heart. And in the New Testament, we have an explanation and an illustration of how a person acts and reacts when he or she is living by the Lord's indwelling life (walking in the Spirit).

For this reason, God's Word is a lamp for our feet, a light on our path (Ps. 119:105).

The more familiar we are with God's written Word, the more familiar we become with how the Living Word—Christ—speaks and acts. This is true for three main reasons:

1. The written Word of God is an expression of God's mind and heart, which is embodied in Christ.
2. Jesus, the Living Word, speaks in the Scriptures—from Genesis to Revelation.
3. The same Spirit that communicates to you (via the Lord's voice) is the same Spirit who inspired the Scriptures (Rom. 8:9–11; 2 Tim. 3:16).

The process whereby our minds become more in tune with God's will is called the renewal of the mind (Rom. 12:2; 2 Cor. 4:16; Eph. 4:23; Col. 3:10). And the means of this renewal is the Word of God.

According to Romans 12:2, the renewal of our minds allows us to discern the Lord's will. In like manner, Hebrews 4:12 describes the Word of God as being sharper than a two-edged sword (NKJV), *dividing* the soul from the spirit. In other words, the Lord's Word separates what comes from us (the soul) from what comes from Him (the Spirit). The "sword of the Spirit"—which is God's written and spoken Word—brings this separation about (Eph. 6:17).

As we digest Scripture, which contains the words of the living God, we come to understand how God thinks, feels, and wants in contrast to what we think, feel, and want.

> Reflect on what I am saying, for the Lord will give you insight into all this. (2 Tim. 2:7)

Our attitudes are shaped by this understanding, making it easier for us to hear the Lord when He speaks to us.

Under the new covenant, the law of God is written in our minds (Heb. 8:10). But our minds still need to be renewed because we have been affected by the fall.

If we offer ourselves to God as living sacrifices, He can renew our minds and we can know the perfect will of God (Rom. 12:1–2). Like a power cleanser, God's Word cleanses our faulty thinking and ideas, setting them in concert with God's will.

The Bible reveals God's ways that are embodied in Christ. The Holy Spirit's job is to show us how to apply those ways to our own lives and situations.

It's also the Spirit's job to *reveal* the message that's contained in the Scriptures to our hearts. For it's possible to read and even memorize parts of the Bible without "hearing" the voice of Jesus within them.

In Acts 13, we are told that the leaders in Jerusalem didn't "know" who Jesus really was (even though they met Him numerous times). Nor did they "know" the voice of the prophets, even though those prophets were read to them every Sabbath.

> For those who dwell in Jerusalem, and their rulers, because they did not know Him, nor even the voices of the Prophets which are

read every Sabbath, have fulfilled them in condemning Him. (Acts 13:27 NKJV)

This text demonstrates that it's one thing to hear the Bible but quite another to "hear" the voice of Jesus in the Scriptures. Or to put it in Paul's language, it's possible to learn the "letter" of the Bible while missing the "Spirit" (2 Cor. 3:6).

Jesus scolded the religious leaders of His day, saying, "You are in error because you do not know the Scriptures or the power of God" (Matt. 22:29). Even though the people Jesus was speaking to here had an academic knowledge of the Scriptures, they didn't really "know" them. Nor did they know God's power, which is another way of describing the Holy Spirit.

So we need both: a knowledge of the Scriptures that is given by the Holy Spirit, and the Holy Spirit's power in our lives.

Some use the word *illumination* to describe the experience of hearing the Lord's voice in Scripture by the Holy Spirit. Suddenly, a text you've read for years takes on a new, wonderful, and personal meaning. In such cases, the Spirit of Jesus has "spoken" to you through His Word.

While it's possible to go off the deep end and confuse the Lord's voice with your own emotions and carnal desires, it's also possible to go off the shallow end and restrict the living voice of God to the letter of the Bible. Both positions are unscriptural and will lead to spiritual loss.

The Lord's voice will always be compatible with the Lord's life that dwells within us and the revelation of God contained in Scripture.

Break Thou the bread of life, dear Lord, to me,
As Thou didst break the loaves beside the sea;
Beyond the sacred page I seek Thee, Lord;
My spirit pants for Thee, O living Word!
—MARY A. LATHBURY[1]

EIGHTEEN

Spiritual Instincts

The voice of the Lord is like a voice, but it's not really a voice.

It's more of an impulse, instinct, or guided intuition.

In the old covenant, God's people responded to Him by trying to follow His law in an external way. This, of course, resulted in failure and condemnation (Rom. 7:1–25; 1 Cor. 15:56; 2 Cor. 3:1–18; Gal. 3:21).

In the new covenant, however, God has written His law on the hearts of His people (2 Cor. 3:3). And we can respond to Him by the inward promptings of the Spirit given to us by the Lord Jesus Himself. Those inward promptings supply the life and the grace to carry out what He says (Rom. 8:1–4).

When we walk in the Spirit of Christ, the moral requirements of the law are fulfilled in us (Matt. 5:17; Rom. 7:4–6). However, "it is not I, but Christ who lives in me" who is doing the work (Gal. 2:20, author's paraphrase).

In that regard, when the voice of the Lord comes to us, it most often comes in the form of our own conscious thoughts, inclinations, and impressions.

The life of Christ within you, then, has a consciousness that either prompts or forbids you to take action. This is what we mean by "spiritual instinct."

In fact, it can rightly be said that when we were "born anew," we heard "the voice of the Son of God" for the first time: "The dead shall hear the voice of the Son of God" (John 5:25 KJV). In another place, Jesus said that we come to Him because the Father draws us and we *hear* Him speaking.

> "No one can come to Me unless the Father who sent Me *draws* him; and I will raise him up on the last day. It is written in the prophets, 'AND THEY SHALL ALL BE TAUGHT OF GOD.' Everyone who has *heard* and learned from the Father, comes to Me." (John 6:44–45 NASB)

You may not have recognized it to be such at the time, but there was an inward "ring" of truth when the gospel message pierced your ears. You "heard" the word of the living God inwardly, which brought your dead spirit to life and gave you new birth.

> For you have been born again, not of perishable seed, but of imperishable, through the living and enduring word of God. (1 Peter 1:23)

> He chose to give us birth through the word of truth, that we might be a kind of firstfruits of all he created. (James 1:18)

> So faith comes from hearing, and hearing by the word of Christ. (Rom. 10:17 NASB)

When God speaks to us in Christ, eternity breaks through time. Beyond the audible, natural, and earthly, the voice of the Son of God—which may or may not employ words—has spoken to us and we inwardly know. Faith is generated in our hearts (Rom. 10:17).

Our Union with Christ

In 1 Corinthians 6:17, Paul made this dramatic statement: "He who is joined to the Lord is one spirit with Him" (NKJV).

Imagine a tea bag being placed into hot water. Slowly, the tea begins to mix with the water, making the tea and the water one.

The same thing happens when the Spirit of Jesus enters your inner being. He joins Himself to your spirit—the deepest part of you—and His life envelops your mind, will, and emotions.

So as a person who has been born from above, you have another life living inside of you. And with that life you have another mind, another feeling, another will, and another consciousness. You have Christ's entire personality dwelling inside of you.

Consequently, when Jesus speaks, what He says typically comes through our own thoughts and judgments. Some refer to this as "a still small voice" (1 Kings 19:12 KJV).

An example is found in 1 Corinthians 7. There Paul said that the Lord didn't give him a specific command on a particular subject, yet he offered his judgment on the matter. And in the process, he was writing inspired Scripture (see 1 Cor. 7:25). Later he made another judgment on a matter, ending his point by saying, "I think that I too have the Spirit of God" (v. 40). In other words, the Lord was speaking to Paul through his own thoughts and judgments.

But that's not all. When Jesus feels, He feels through our emotions.

God can testify how I long for all of you with the affection of Christ Jesus. (Phil. 1:8)

And when Jesus wills, He wills through our volition (will).

For it is God who works in you to will and to act in order to fulfill his good purpose. (Phil. 2:13)

Since the Lord is so connected with your human spirit—the deepest part of you—His voice comes through your thoughts, your feelings, and your desires.

The trick, therefore, is to discern when your thoughts, your feelings, and your will are reflecting the Lord's mind, feelings, and will rather than your own.

The Simplicity of Hearing the Lord

Unfortunately, when some Christians speak about how God communicates with them, they give the impression that He talks audibly or by some other spectacular method.

The truth is that even among the most mature believers, the Lord most often speaks through the still small voice of our thoughts, emotions, or desires.

Since Christ indwells the deepest part of your being by the Holy Spirit, Jesus is nearer to you than the breath is to your mouth (Rom. 10:6–13).

In fact, Paul said that if you say, "Jesus is Lord" in true faith, the Holy Spirit inspired you to say those words: "No one can say, 'Jesus is Lord,' except by the Holy Spirit" (1 Cor. 12:3).

The Lord's speaking, then, usually doesn't come with fireworks, explosions, thunder, lightning, or any other dramatic and spectacular event, as we can learn from the experience of the prophet Elijah:

> The LORD said, "Go out and stand on the mountain in the presence of the LORD, for the LORD is about to pass by." Then a great and powerful wind tore the mountains apart and shattered the rocks before the LORD, but the LORD was not in the wind. After the wind there was an earthquake, but the LORD was not in the earthquake. After the earthquake came a fire, but the LORD was not in the fire. And after the fire came a gentle whisper. (1 Kings 19:11–12)

While the Holy Spirit sometimes comes to us like a rushing mighty wind (Acts 2:2–4), most of the time He comes in much less assuming ways, like a gentle dove (Luke 3:22). In our observation, those who insist that God usually makes Himself known in spectacular ways are revealing their spiritual immaturity as well as their doubt (Matt. 16:1ff.).

In short, when we are following our spiritual instincts, we are following the Lord's voice. And in so doing, our very steps are ordered by Jesus Himself.

> The Lord directs the steps of the godly.
>
> He delights in every detail of their lives. (Ps. 37:23 NLT)

What Does It Look Like?

In our last chapter, we learned that the voice of the Lord most often comes through our thoughts, emotions, or desires.

The best way to describe the Lord's voice is an impulse or instinct that we recognize through our minds, wills, or emotions. But what does it look like?

We could provide a multitude of examples, even filling another book with them. But here are a few to give you an idea.

A man was once having a fancy dinner, celebrating an achievement in his life. As he pulled away from the restaurant, he saw a woman in the parking lot, holding up a sign that read: "I'm homeless and hungry. Please help."

The man continued to drive toward his home, but he had a gnawing impression inside his heart. He thought about the wonderful meal he was just blessed to purchase and enjoy. Then he thought about the woman who was standing on the side of the road, hungry.

The impression kept coming to him. It wouldn't go away.

As he was on his way home, he gave in to the instinct. He made a U-turn and drove back to the parking lot. He found the homeless woman still there and gave her a twenty-dollar bill with a word of blessing from God. The woman was both surprised and elated. The inner stirring stopped; the burden lifted.

In this case, the man heard no voice. It was just a constant impression.

Or maybe you are occupied with some task, like mowing the lawn, washing dishes, clearing out your garage, or mopping the floor. And suddenly, the thought of a person you know is laid upon your heart.

You feel a burden to pray for that individual. Or perhaps call to check on him or her. This is the Lord's voice directing you to reach out to someone, either in prayer or another way.

Or perhaps you feel a strong inclination or tendency to spend more time with the Lord. This is His voice drawing you toward His presence.

These are some of the subtle ways in which the Lord Jesus communicates with us by His Spirit. But so often, we ignore them because we write them off as being our own thoughts or desires.

Let us repeat: the Lord's voice is *like* a voice in that it gives us instruction, but it's not really a voice. It's more of an instinct.

And the more we grow into the likeness of Christ, the more we know by instinct what the Lord wants in a given situation, rather than having to be told by some external means.

So be alert and attentive to what's happening in your life, including your own heart and mind.

Be attentive to what's happening in your circumstances.

Be alert to what others are saying to you.

Look for the Lord's voice in the mundane events of everyday life.

As Elizabeth Barrett Browning aptly wrote:

> Earth's crammed with Heaven,
> And every common bush afire with God;
> But only he who sees takes off his shoes.
> The rest sit around it and pluck blueberries.[1]

If we aren't expecting the Lord to lead and guide us each day, we'll find ourselves walking past countless burning bushes without noticing.

TWENTY

Wisdom

In Colossians 2:3, Paul said that in Christ "are hidden all the treasures of wisdom and knowledge." Even more striking, Paul declared that Jesus Christ *is* the wisdom of God (1 Cor. 1:24).

Because Christ indwells you, His wisdom is available to you.

> It is because of him that you are in Christ Jesus, who has become for us wisdom from God. (1 Cor. 1:30)

Very often, when we are seeking the Lord's voice, He is wanting us to exercise wisdom. Put another way, He wants us to make a wise choice. Psalm 32:8–9 underscores the point:

> I will instruct you and teach you in the way you should go;
> I will guide you with My eye.
> Do not be like the horse or like the mule,
> Which have no understanding,
> Which must be harnessed with bit and bridle,
> Else they will not come near you. (NKJV)

The horse and mule have no understanding. They are without

discernment or judgment. Consequently, they must be pulled with the bit and bridle. They must be given orders for their every move.

But the Lord tells His people, "I will teach you which way to go. Don't be like the horse and mule, which have no understanding."

One of the ways the Lord guides us is by giving us wisdom and understanding.

> Brethren, do not be children in understanding; however, in malice be babes, but in understanding be mature. (1 Cor. 14:20 NKJV)

The Corinthians were living like natural people in the world (the unsaved). They were spiritual babes and couldn't understand the things of the Holy Spirit (1 Cor. 3:1–3).

Paul told them that the spiritually mature are those who are able to exercise discernment and judgment (1 Cor. 2:6–3:3). So instead of giving us orders and commands at every turn, the Lord often wants us to exercise wisdom. James gave us a wonderful promise about this:

> If any of you lacks wisdom, let him ask of God, who gives to all liberally and without reproach, and it will be given to him. But let him ask in faith, with no doubting, for he who doubts is like a wave of the sea driven and tossed by the wind. For let not that man suppose that he will receive anything from the Lord; he is a double-minded man, unstable in all his ways. (James 1:5–8 NKJV)

Precise Guidance

The Lord doesn't always give us precise guidance. Nor does He dictate every move we should make. Rather, He expects us to mature in His life and make choices that reflect His own character.

If a parent specified what a child was to do at every moment of every day, the child's growth would be stunted. Consequently, responsible parents guide their children, giving them moral instruction, then hoping that they will make wise decisions for themselves.

Just think: How many of us wake up in the morning and ask the Lord how many times we're supposed to stroke when we brush our teeth, or what shirt to put on, or what to eat for breakfast?

Or how many of us ask the Lord what to order when we're at a restaurant when the waitress or waiter asks us for our order?

You may retort, "Well, that's crazy. I just choose."

Yes, but the Lord often gives you the same latitude with other things in life. As long as your decision is within the parameters of His will, the choice is yours.

There isn't always one choice that represents the Lord's will. *In fact, in many respects, the Lord's will is more like a parking lot than a train track.*

Again, a child will never develop into a responsible adult if she or he is always told what to do. God is not after robots. Nor is He after human beings who jump at His every beck and call like dogs that have been conditioned to do so. The Lord is after a people who have His mind, who think as He does, anticipating His ways and desires.

This insight has freed many Christians from obsessing with great anxiety over "the right thing to do" in a given situation. For in most cases, they know what the right thing to do is.

It's like the story of the man who was stranded at sea and prayed for God to rescue him. A ship came by and the captain yelled, "Do you want help?" The stranded man replied, "No thanks. I prayed and God will deliver me. I have faith."

Then a sailboat came by and the man in the boat asked the same thing. The man's reply was the same: "I've prayed. God will deliver me."

Then a man in a canoe came by and asked the man if he wanted help. His reply was the same.

The moral of the story is that God answered the man, but He did so in a way that the man didn't expect. So the man stayed stranded, failing to discern the Lord's will.

Divine Wisdom Granted

When the church in Jerusalem met its first crisis (Acts 6:1–4), the apostles said, "Pick seven men among you who are spiritual and who have wisdom" (v. 3, authors' paraphrase).

In the Corinthian church, there were some men taking others in the church to the secular courts to resolve personal conflicts (1 Cor. 6:4–5). What was Paul's solution? "Is there not a wise man among you who can settle these disputes?" (v. 5, authors' paraphrase).

When Paul gave instruction regarding the elders in his letters to Timothy and Titus, he said that the elders are those who are "sensible" (1 Tim. 3:2 HCSB; Titus 1:8 NASB) and "discreet" (1 Tim. 3:2 DARBY; Titus 1:8 DARBY). In other words, they should possess wisdom and sound judgment.

Wisdom is not natural reasoning independent of God. Wisdom comes out of dependence upon the Lord. So any piece of authentic wisdom that you receive comes from your Lord, for He is Wisdom embodied.

Consider the following exhortations to exercise wise judgment:

Do not judge according to appearance, but *judge* with righteous *judgment.* (John 7:24 NKJV)

Test all things; hold fast what is good. Abstain from every form of evil. (1 Thess. 5:21–22 NKJV)

Consider what I say, and may the Lord give you *understanding* in all things. (2 Tim. 2:7 NKJV)

See then that you walk circumspectly, not as fools but as *wise*, redeeming the time, because the days are evil. Therefore do not be unwise, but *understand* what the will of the Lord is. (Eph. 5:15–17 NKJV)

I speak as to *wise* men; *judge* for yourselves what I say. (1 Cor. 10:15 NKJV)

Judge among yourselves. (1 Cor. 11:13 NKJV)

Let two or three prophets speak, and let the others *judge*. (1 Cor. 14:29 NKJV)

As a person who has God's life inside of you—which is the birthright of every Christian—you possess an inner compass pointing to the Lord's will at all times. Consequently, the Lord's speaking is often found through the voice of Wisdom, which is the voice of Jesus Himself.

TWENTY-ONE

The Body of Christ

In 1 Corinthians 2:16, Paul talks about having the mind of Christ. The "mind of Christ" points to a mind-set, a way of thinking.

When Paul penned these words, he wasn't speaking about an individual having the mind of Christ. He was talking to the body of Christ in Corinth. He was saying, "You—collectively and together—have the mind of Christ."

This brings us to yet another way in which Jesus speaks to us today. In 1 Corinthians 12:1–3, Paul wrote:

Now concerning spiritual gifts, brothers, I do not want you to be uninformed. You know that when you were pagans you were led astray to mute idols, however you were led. Therefore I want you to understand that no one speaking in the Spirit of God ever says "Jesus is accursed!" and no one can say "Jesus is Lord" except in the Holy Spirit. (ESV)

Here Paul told the Corinthian Christians that they were led by mute idols. Before the Corinthians met the living God, they were following pagan idols who didn't have the power of speech.

In this text, Paul was essentially saying:

Remember how you served mute idols? Well, now you serve a God who speaks, and He speaks through you and your fellow members of the body of Christ. For example, when you say, "Jesus is Lord," God's own Spirit is speaking through you. There are varieties of spiritual gifts, but it's the same Spirit. There are varieties of ministries, but it's the same Lord. And there are varieties of effects, but it's the same God who is working through them all. The one true God speaks through a variety of different ways via His one body. (vv. 2–6, paraphrased)

Jesus Christ speaks through His body, the church. Hence, Paul said in 1 Corinthians 2:9–10: "However, as it is written: 'What no eye has seen, what no ear has heard, and what no human mind has conceived'— the things God has prepared for those who love him—these are the things God has revealed to us by his Spirit. The Spirit searches all things, even the deep things of God."

Consider the following:

"No eye has seen." He's speaking of a single eye. The solo eye has not seen.

"No ear has heard." The individual ear has not heard.

"No human mind has conceived [what] God has prepared." No single mind has received.

Now listen to Paul in 1 Corinthians 2:16: "For 'who has known the mind of the LORD that he may instruct Him?'" (NKJV).

The answer is obvious. No individual has God's full mind on any subject.

Paul followed that comment with this remarkable statement: "But we [plural] have the mind of Christ." We, corporately—as His body— possess the mind of Christ!

The mind of Christ is discoverable. Jesus has the power of speech, and He desires to speak and reveal His thoughts to you.

But the full mind of Christ is a corporate discovery and a corporate pursuit. It's not the property of any individual. It's the property of the body of Christ.

This is one of the reasons why we cannot recognize the voice of Jesus at certain times in our lives. The Lord is wanting us to rely on the other members of the body to discern it.

Remember when Paul came to Jesus on the Damascus road? Jesus told Paul that he would receive further instructions through one of the men in the church in Damascus named Ananias (Acts 9; 22:10–16).

Jesus could have easily told Paul everything he needed to know directly. But He chose to give Paul further insight through one of the members of the body. This is the principle of the body of Christ at work.

A young man who graduated from high school was planning on going on a mission trip with his friend. The young man was conflicted about going because there was a new church being planted in his town, and he didn't want to miss out on the foundational stages. In his conflict, he asked some of the men in his church to pray with him and ask God to reveal His mind concerning the mission trip.

The men got together and began seeking the Lord. After a bit of silence, all of the men said that they didn't feel peace about the young man going on the mission trip. They sensed it was the mind of Christ for him to stay in town.

The young man yielded to the direction of his fellow brethren and opted out of the mission trip. Tragically, the plane he would have been on crashed and everyone onboard died.

There will be times in your life where you will have trouble discerning the Lord's mind. At such times, lean on the body of Christ for His direction. It could end up saving your life.

In the multitude of counselors there is safety. (Prov. 11:14 NKJV)

In the mouth of two or three witnesses shall every word be established. (2 Cor. 13:1 KJV)

TWENTY-TWO

Visions and Dreams

Under the old covenant, God spoke to His prophets in visions—mental images that come into a person's mind—and dreams (Num. 12:6). When visions and dreams were absent in Israel, it indicated that the nation had strayed from God (1 Sam. 3:1; Lam. 2:9; Mic. 3:6–7).

With the coming of the Holy Spirit under the new covenant, however, the Lord broadened the scope of visions and dreams to all of His people (Acts 9:10–13; 10:9–19; 16:9; 18:9; 2 Cor. 12:1).

> "'In the last days, God says,
>   I will pour out my Spirit on all people.
> Your sons and daughters will prophesy,
>   your young men will see visions,
>   your old men will dream dreams.'" (Acts 2:17)

When I was a young believer, the Lord would frequently speak to me in dreams and visions. The dreams usually had to be interpreted, which provoked me to seek the Lord for understanding.

The visions given were often simple. One time while I was praying, a picture of a man preaching appeared on the screen of my mind. In the vision, the preacher said, "Turn to Psalm 40:1." I looked up that text and found a much-needed word of encouragement for the time.

In the New Testament, visions either were plain (Acts 9:10–12; 10:3–8; 18:9–10) or needed to be interpreted (Acts 10:9–18; 16:9–10). The same is true with dreams throughout the Bible.

As I matured in my faith, however, visions and dreams that originated from the Lord drastically decreased.

The late Dallas Willard observed that the greater the maturity of the listener, the lesser the role played by visions and dreams. Going further, Willard believed that a person who is mainly led by God through visions and dreams is less developed in spiritual life than he or she should be.[1]

The authors of this book agree with Willard. In our experience, visions and dreams are like training wheels that help us grow into the place where we are able to follow our spiritual instincts.

Even so, sometimes God will use dreams to get our attention when we've turned a deaf ear to His voice (Job 33:13–18).

TWENTY-THREE

The Audible Voice

It's common for us to assume that every time God spoke in the Old and New Testaments, He did so audibly. But this is a misguided assumption.

When Samuel first heard the voice of the Lord, *Eli didn't hear it at all* (1 Sam. 3:1–10).

When Jesus heard the voice of His Father from heaven, *the crowd heard only a noise of some kind* (John 12:27–29).

When Paul heard the voice of Jesus on the road to Damascus, *the others around him heard a sound, but no intelligible voice* (Acts 9:5–7; 22:9).

In those cases, the audible voice of God was only heard by the person to whom God was speaking. The rest either heard nothing or a kind of noise. The point is that God didn't always speak audibly in the Bible in the sense that every person within earshot distance heard it.

In other cases, the Lord certainly spoke audibly wherein others who were around heard it (Matt. 17:5; 2 Peter 1:17–18). Interestingly, though, when mortals heard the audible voice of God, they were typically terrified (Ex. 20:18–20; Deut. 4:36; 5:23–29; Matt. 17:6).

Yet even in the Old Testament, the audible voice of God was quite rare. God spoke audibly on a regular basis to only some of His servants (Ex. 19:9; Num. 12:6–8).

Neither of us has ever heard the audible voice of God. However, we have interviewed many people who claimed to have heard it. And in every case, the people ended up admitting that it wasn't audible in the sense that their physical ears heard it. Instead, it was so strong and so clear in their spirits that it was *like* an audible voice.

Taking the whole of the New Testament together, it is our belief that when the Spirit spoke to someone in the book of Acts, it wasn't audible, but internal.

We don't doubt that God may speak to some people audibly on rare occasion. But this isn't His normative way of speaking, either in Scripture or today.

His primary way of speaking to us is through the means we've covered so far. And there is yet one other way . . .

TWENTY-FOUR

The Conscience

So far, we've seen that the Lord speaks through Scripture, He speaks through our spiritual instincts, He speaks through wisdom, He speaks through visions and dreams, and He speaks through His body.

But there is yet another way that He speaks to us: the human conscience.

In Acts 24:16, Paul declared, "This being so, I myself always strive to have a conscience without offense toward God and men" (NKJV).

In Romans, Paul wrote, "They demonstrate that God's law is written in their hearts, for their own conscience and thoughts either accuse them or tell them they are doing right" (Rom. 2:15 NLT). And later, "I am speaking the truth in Christ—I am not lying; my conscience bears me witness in the Holy Spirit" (Rom. 9:1 ESV).

Each one of us has a conscience, an inward monitor that goes off when we step out of God's will and bears witness with the Holy Spirit when we are walking in His will.

In Romans 9, Paul was about to make a statement that sounded like a lie. He then pointed to his conscience as a witness that he was telling the truth (v. 1). The voice of the Lord through the conscience, then, will alert us if we are speaking truthfully, deceiving, or exaggerating. The conscience, then, is like an internal alarm. Anything that offends your conscience is something to stay clear of. Anything that your conscience allows is morally permissible for you.

The exception is if you have violated your conscience so many times that it ceases to operate. The Bible calls this state having a "seared" conscience (1 Tim. 4:2).

When seeking to hear the voice of the Lord, we have been given five lighthouses:

1. The testimony of Scripture (2 Tim. 3)
2. The inward instincts of the Holy Spirit written on our minds and hearts (Rom. 8; Gal. 5; Heb. 8)
3. Wisdom
4. The dictates of our conscience[1]
5. The body of Christ

All of these lighthouses enable us to fulfill Paul's words in Ephesians 5:17: "Therefore do not be unwise, but understand what the will of the Lord is" (NKJV).

TWENTY-FIVE

Another Look at Jesus

As we pointed out in *Jesus Manifesto*, what the Father was to Jesus, Jesus is to us. The way that Jesus lived His life, then, is a model for how we are to live it. This includes the subject of hearing God.

> He who says he abides in Him [Christ] ought himself also *to walk just as He [Christ] walked.* (1 John 2:6 NKJV)

Getting back to the matter of spiritual instincts, a consistent theme throughout the Gospels is the contrast between the Pharisees and Jesus. The same contrast can be seen between Jesus and His disciples (before Christ ascended and filled them with His Spirit).

According to the Gospels, the Pharisees reasoned while Jesus perceived.

> But there was certain of the scribes sitting there, and *reasoning* in their hearts, Why doth this man thus speak blasphemies? who can forgive sins but God only? And immediately when Jesus *perceived* in his spirit that they so reasoned within themselves, he said unto them, Why reason ye these things in your hearts? (Mark 2:6–8 KJV)

> Then there arose a *reasoning* among them, which of them should be greatest. And Jesus, *perceiving* the thought of their heart, took a child, and set him by him. (Luke 9:46–47 KJV)

And they *reasoned* among themselves, saying, It is because we have taken no bread. Which when Jesus *perceived*, he said unto them, O ye of little faith, why reason ye among yourselves, because ye have brought no bread? (Matt. 16:7–8 KJV)

When Jesus therefore *perceived* that they would come and take him by force, to make him a king, he departed again into a mountain himself alone. (John 6:15 KJV)

Spiritual perception has to do with following the internal witness inside our hearts by the Holy Spirit—it's another way of describing the act of recognizing the Lord's voice.

Some have suggested that it was because He was the Son of God that Jesus heard the Father's supernatural voice. But this is not true. Jesus, while fully divine, lived as a human being anointed and indwelt by the Holy Spirit. In this way, He truly became our model and an example.

... how *God anointed Jesus of Nazareth with the Holy Spirit and power,* and how he went around doing good and healing all who were under the power of the devil, because God was with him. (Acts 10:38)

Though he was God,
    he did not think of equality with God
    as something to cling to.
Instead, *he gave up his divine privileges* [Greek: He emptied Himself];
    he took the humble position of a slave
    and was born as a human being. (Phil. 2:6–7 NLT)

As the living Father hath sent me, and *I live by the Father:* so he that eateth me, even *he shall live by me.* (John 6:57 KJV)

Because Jesus was fully human, He hungered (Matt. 4:2), thirsted (John 19:28), and became tired (John 4:6). He also *grew* in wisdom, learning things by natural means (Luke 2:52; John 4:1–3). As "the Son of Man," He did not possess exhaustive knowledge. For example, He didn't know the precise time of His second coming (Matt. 24:36).

Jesus' display of supernatural knowledge and power came by the anointing of the Holy Spirit (Isa. 11:1–5; 42:1–4; 61:1–3; Luke 4:1, 14–21; Acts 10:38).

In that light, consider the following texts that describe how Jesus heard the voice of His Father. This includes the various ways we've described thus far—through spiritual instinct, wisdom, visions, and so forth.

"The Son can do nothing by himself; he can do only *what he sees his Father doing*, because whatever the Father does the Son also does." (John 5:19)

"By myself I can do nothing; *I judge only as I hear*, and my judgment is just, for I seek not to please myself but him who sent me." (John 5:30)

"But he who sent me is trustworthy, and *what I have heard from him* I tell the world." (John 8:26)

"I do nothing on my own but speak just *what the Father has taught me*." (John 8:28)

"I am telling you *what I have seen in the Father's presence*." (John 8:38)

"For I did not speak *on my own, but the Father* who sent me commanded me to say all that I have spoken." (John 12:49)

"Whatever I say is *just what the Father has told me to say*." (John 12:50)

"Don't you believe that I am in the Father, and that *the Father is in me*? The words I say to you I do not speak on my own authority. Rather, *it is the Father, living in me, who is doing his work*." (John 14:10)

157

"And I will ask the Father, and he will give you another advocate to help you and be with you forever—the Spirit of truth. The world cannot accept him, because it neither sees him nor knows him. But you know him, for *he* [the Spirit] lives with you *and will be in you.* I will not leave you as orphans; *I [Jesus] will come to you.* Before long, the world will not see me anymore, but you will see me. Because I live, you also will live. On that day you will realize that I am in my Father, and you are in me, *and I am in you.*" (John 14:16–20)

Then Jesus was *led by the Spirit* into the wilderness to be tempted by the devil. (Matt. 4:1)

The Spirit then compelled Jesus to go into the wilderness. (Mark 1:12 NLT)

"Therefore the wisdom of God also said, 'I will send them prophets and apostles, and some of them they will kill and persecute.'" (Luke 11:49 NKJV)

But He answered and said, "It is written, . . ."
     Jesus said to him, "It is written again, . . .
     "For it is written, . . ." (Matt. 4:4, 7, 10 NKJV)

It is clear from these texts that Jesus had a conversational relationship with His Father that was mostly internal. In other words, He would often commune with His Father in His mind and heart without saying anything aloud.

This comment by Jesus makes this point clear: "Father, thank you for hearing me. You always hear me, but *I said it out loud for the sake of all these people standing here,* so that they will believe you sent me" (John 11:41–42 NLT).

Another example is found in John 12: "Then a voice came from heaven, 'I have glorified it, and will glorify it again.' The crowd that was there and heard it said it had thundered; others said an angel had

spoken to him. Jesus said, 'This voice was for your benefit, not mine'"
(vv. 28–30).

Because of Christ's death and resurrection, the only begotten Son of
God became the firstborn Son among many brothers and sisters (Rom.
8:29).

Birth is the impartation of life. So when Jesus rose again from the
dead, He became a life-giving spirit (1 Cor. 15:45). He has imparted the
divine life into you, so you have become born from above and made the
children of God.

It is for this reason that we see the disciples in the book of Acts doing
many of the same things Jesus did during His earthly ministry, including
healings, casting out of demons, miracles, knowing things supernatu-
rally, and being led by the voice of the Lord.

Again, what the Father was to Jesus by the Spirit, Jesus is to you by
the same Spirit. Therefore you also can have a conversational relationship with the Lord that includes internal fellowship as well as praying
out loud.

TWENTY-SIX

Four Ways to
Recognize the Lord's Voice

We've seen that the Lord primarily speaks to us through the Scriptures and by our spiritual instincts, which register in our minds, wills, or emotions. He also speaks to us through the body of Christ, through our conscience, and through wisdom, visions, and dreams.

So the question to be answered now is: *How do I discern the difference between when the Lord speaks and when the thought comes from some other source?*

The story in 1 Samuel 3:1–11 is the summary witness that when the Lord speaks to us, we don't always recognize it. So we need an Eli to help us recognize and respond to the Lord's speaking. That's precisely why we wrote this book.

In our own experience, we've discovered that there are four chief ways we can discern the Lord's voice from our own or that of others:

- the content
- the disposition
- the confidence
- the impression

Let's look at each one.

The Content

When the Lord speaks to you through your thoughts, it doesn't "sound" any different from your own thoughts. What's different, however, is *the content* of those thoughts.

Content from the Lord will always be in harmony with Scripture. It will never contradict it. The Lord's present speaking will always be consistent with what He's said in the past. More specifically, it will bear the marks of giving and self-sacrifice, which is love—the love that fulfills the Law and the Prophets. (The phrase "the Law and the Prophets" is shorthand for the entire Old Testament.)

Remember, the very nature of Jesus Christ is love. According to the Bible, love is treating others the way we want to be treated and benefiting others at the expense of ourselves (Matt. 7:12; Luke 9:23–24; Rom. 15:1–3; 1 John 3:17; 4:16).

Because Christ lives in us, we are divinely and intuitively taught how to love:

> Now about your love for one another we do not need to write to you, for you yourselves have been taught by God to love each other. (1 Thess. 4:9)

> God's love has been poured out into our hearts through the Holy Spirit, who has been given to us. (Rom. 5:5)

So if the content of your thoughts is leading you to deny yourself and give to others, it is consistent with the Lord's voice.[1]

In addition, the content will often shed light on the person of Christ Himself, revealing His nature, His character, His loveliness, and so forth, because the Holy Spirit has come to reveal and glorify Jesus (John 15:26; 16:14). For example, see Revelation 1–3, when Jesus spoke to the seven churches in Asia Minor. In each case, the Lord revealed a particular aspect of Himself before every word of encouragement or correction.

The Disposition

When the Lord speaks to us, the disposition that accompanies it will never be one of hastiness, arrogance, jealousy, anger, or anxiety.

Instead, the Lord's speaking comes to us with a spirit of peacefulness and goodwill. James gave us a perfect description of the disposition of the Lord's voice when he wrote, "But the wisdom from above is first of all pure. It is also peace loving, gentle at all times, and willing to yield to others. It is full of mercy and the fruit of good deeds. It shows no favoritism and is always sincere" (James 3:17 NLT).

Jesus is the same today, yesterday, and forever (Heb. 13:8). When Christ was on earth as the Son of Man, He was so gentle that His voice couldn't be heard above the street chatter (Matt. 12:19).

In the same way, when the Lord speaks to us today, He doesn't shout. He gently whispers to us, even when His words enlighten or prick our conscience.

His overtures are peaceful; His speaking, meek.

In that connection, Jesus never accuses or condemns His true followers. Condemnation and accusation are the marks of the enemy's voice. Note that the word *devil* means "slanderer," because his nature is to persistently accuse the children of God (Rev. 12:10).

By contrast, when Jesus points out something in our lives that He wants us to deal with, His correction comes with love and hope.

The Confidence

When the Lord speaks to us through our thoughts, emotions, or desires, what He says possesses "the ring of truth." There is an inward witness that resonates within us. In other words, we have confidence—or faith—to believe that the Lord is speaking to us (see chapters 11–13).

The Lord's voice, then, is most often revealed by an inward knowing. There is a confidence present that the Lord is speaking, much the same way you know you belong to God by the inward consciousness of the Holy Spirit.

> The Spirit himself bears witness with our spirit that we are children of God. (Rom. 8:16 ESV)

If you have no faith to believe that a thought, feeling, desire, or impulse is coming from the Lord, then it probably isn't.

The Impression

There is a certain impression that the Lord's voice makes upon us.

First, His speaking will be accompanied by life (inspiration) and peace (serenity) in our hearts.

> But the mind governed by the Spirit is life and peace. (Rom. 8:6)

> For the word of God is alive and active. (Heb. 4:12)

So when determining if the Lord is speaking to you, look for the sense of life and peace within. The effect of His speaking will often be rest, peace, quiet joy, and reassurance.

Regarding the sense of life, there will be an accompanying energy or enthusiasm when the Lord speaks to us. Life is energy. The Greek word for "enthusiasm" means "possessed by God." It refers to a strong excitement or emotion that compels one to act.

In the opposite manner, whenever we step out of God's will, we will have a sense of death within us. Our spirits will also be troubled and disturbed.

This is why the perpetually disobedient Christian is the most miserable person on the planet. That individual is holding some attitude or behavior that runs contrary to the life and nature of God that indwells him or her.

Remember: Christ lives in you. So when He approves or disapproves of an attitude or behavior, it will register in your consciousness. You will inwardly know something is incompatible with Christ. Because Christ is our life (Col. 3:4), we can sense His reactions and responses within us.

As we saw in the Road to Emmaus story, sometimes when the Lord speaks to us, we will experience "Jesus heartburn" (see Luke 24:32, as well as chapter 2 of this book). Our hearts will be warmed by what He reveals.

Another impression we may have is insight. The Lord's speaking often holds insights that exceed the normal capacity of our natural minds. You may have the keen impression that the idea isn't yours because you're not smart enough to have come up with it on your own.

In addition, often when the Lord speaks to us, the prompting will stay with us. We can't shake it. It's almost like a gnawing or a burden. It will not be overpowering, but it will remain with us.

So a good test to discern whether an impression is from the Lord or not is to write it down and leave it alone for a while. If the thought, feeling, desire, or impulse is still with you after some time has passed, and it contains the other three marks of His voice, you've likely heard it from the Lord.

Keep in mind that we sometimes don't understand the full significance of what the Lord is saying to us at the time.

Peter, for instance, declared with confidence by the Spirit's revelation that Jesus was the Messiah, the Son of the living God (Matt. 16:16). But Peter didn't fully understand what his confession meant. Not long after, Jesus had to rebuke Peter, alleging that Satan was speaking through him (Matt. 16:23).

Sometimes the Lord will impress upon our minds a fragment or even a sentence. And at first blush, we won't fully understand its meaning.

Why would the Lord speak to us partially at times rather than plainly? Very simply: He wants us to keep seeking Him for insight. Jesus often spoke in mysteries when He was on earth, desiring that His disciples ask Him for fuller understanding. He does the same thing today.

In 1 Corinthians 13, Paul clearly said that both prophecy and knowledge are partial in this life (v. 9). The same is true with the voice of the Lord, which is related to both prophecy and knowledge.

Other times, however, He will speak fully and clearly.

So there you have it. There are four characteristics that will help you determine whether you are hearing the Lord's voice:

1. The content of what's said
2. The disposition that accompanies it
3. The confidence we have that it's the Lord
4. The impression it makes upon us

We distinguish human voices by the characteristics of their speech. It's no different with the divine voice.

It should go without saying that a final indication is the fruit of what's being said. If we follow the Lord's true voice, it will ultimately produce good fruit (Isa. 55:11 NLT).

The phrase "good fruit" assumes that what we believe the Lord has spoken proves itself to be accurate. For example, if the Lord truly speaks to us about the future, it will come to pass. And if He shows us something about another individual, it will be accurate. If not, then we have confused His voice with our own or another source, because God cannot lie (Titus 1:2).

TWENTY-SEVEN

Practical Steps to Receiving
a Word from the Lord

As we have stressed already, the Lord is always speaking to His children. So we should strive to remain in a posture of constant listening, even while we're busy and active.

There are special times, however—times of crisis or lack of clarity—when we may need His specific guidance on a matter. Think of the difference between being in frequent communication with your friend and calling your friend when you have an emergency.

Let us first point out that there is no technique, method, or gimmick to hearing the Lord speak to you. However, in our experience, we've found these practical guidelines to prove helpful when we are in need of the Lord's mind on a matter:

1. Bring the matter before the Lord with specific prayer. Ask Him to show you His will in the matter. With childlike faith, *expect* Him to reveal His mind to you. Don't put any restrictions on how He can speak to you.

   Tell Him something like, "Lord, I am listening. Please speak to me through any means You wish: my thoughts, my friends, a book, an article, a recorded talk, my circumstances, or any unexpected means."

2. For the next hour or two, engage in some kind of activity that doesn't occupy your mind. Things like driving, walking, or exercising will work. In this way, you are giving space for the Lord to speak to you.

3. If, during that time, a thought or impression comes to you in relation to the matter, write it down.

4. If no answer comes, don't be alarmed. Go on with your business, still expecting Him to reveal His mind to you. Continue to pay attention to your feelings, thoughts, and surrounding circumstances.

   Continue with a posture of being attentive and listening.

   Sometimes in a few days—or weeks, even—you may stumble across an article, a book, a social media update, a conversation with a friend, a film, or a recorded message wherein God answers your very question. This is quite common.

5. Resist the urge to play "Bible roulette" or use other techniques wherein you try to force an answer from God (see chapter 38). You don't have to strain and struggle to hear the Lord. He wants to speak to you.

6. If time goes by and you still haven't received an answer, you may want to discuss it with some friends who know the Lord and are mature in Him, asking them to pray with you. In other words, depend on the body of Christ.

7. If the issue is particularly important, you may want to take three days to fast. The most effective fasts are water-only fasts, but we suggest you speak to your doctor if you are on certain medications or you have a condition like low blood sugar, in which case a fast can harm your health.

   We don't have time or space to discuss fasting, but in short, fasting weakens the body (and the flesh) and sharpens your spiritual senses. This is one of the reasons why fasts are so powerful throughout the Bible.

8. If after sufficient time has passed, and you still have received no direction, the reason is most likely one of the following:

You already know the answer deep in your heart:

> As for you, the anointing you received from him remains in you, and you do not need anyone to teach you. But as his anointing teaches you about all things and as that anointing is real, not counterfeit—just as it has taught you, remain in him. (1 John 2:27)

The anointing in this text refers to the inward movement and activity of the Lord within us, as in the spiritual instincts that we discussed earlier.

Consider walking into an extremely cold room. No one has to tell you to keep your jacket on. You know inwardly by the temperature. The same is true if you walked outside in the blazing Florida sun. No one has to tell you to remove your coat.

It's the same with the Lord's anointing within us. Sometimes we just *know* what we are to do by the anointing of His indwelling life.

> For with you is the fountain of life;
> in your light we see light. (Ps. 36:9)

> The human spirit is the lamp of the LORD
> that sheds light on one's inmost being. (Prov. 20:27)

The Spirit searches all things, even the deep things of God. For who knows a person's thoughts except their own spirit within them? In the same way no one knows the thoughts of God except the Spirit of God. (1 Cor. 2:10–11)

Again, we believe hearing the Lord's voice is a constant. God often speaks to us without initiating or asking. So we should always cultivate an attitude of listening.

TWENTY-EIGHT

Take Time for Quiet

If you're constantly bombarding your mind with the ideas, opinions, and thoughts of others, it may be difficult for you to hear the still small voice of Jesus through the clatter.

Consider these texts that encourage us to times of quiet:

"Be still, and know that I am God." (Ps. 46:10)

For God alone my soul waits in silence;
    from him comes my salvation. (Ps. 62:1 ESV)

Let all that I am wait quietly before God,
    for my hope is in him. (Ps. 62:5 NLT)

For thus says the Lord GOD, the Holy One of Israel:
    "In returning and rest you shall be saved;
    In quietness and confidence shall be your strength."
    But you would not. (Isa. 30:15 NKJV)

Surely I have composed and quieted my soul;
Like a weaned child rests against his mother,
My soul is like a weaned child within me. (Ps. 131:2 NASB)

Very often, we are too busy with our own efforts, interests, problems, and ambitions to hear the voice of the Lord. This was true with Saul of Tarsus, and Jesus had to smite him to the ground for Saul to hear Him speak.

So carve out time in your busy schedule to turn down the volume and posture your heart to be still before the Lord amid the carnival of distracting demands.

This doesn't mean that you cause your mind to go blank or empty. Instead, quiet your heart and focus your attention on Jesus, waiting quietly upon Him. For in order to hear the still small voice, we likewise should become still.

In the next three chapters, we'll give you some practical ideas on how to successfully take time for quiet.

TWENTY-NINE

Hearing the Voice in the Morning

Hearing the Lord's voice clearly is derived from cultivating a life of intimacy with Jesus. By learning how to commune with the Lord in prayer and by having our minds renewed by His written Word, we are able to discern what is compatible with His life and nature.

In that regard, through the Old and New Testaments, the morning has always held a special place in hearing from the Lord.

Recall that God gave His people manna in the mornings. And when the sun came up, the manna melted away (Ex. 16:21). This piece of biblical history is an encouragement to begin each day turning our hearts to the Lord and receiving the manna, if you please.

However, we shouldn't leave the Lord in our "quiet time" only to go about our day without giving Him a thought. Rather, we should nurture a conversational relationship with the Lord all throughout the day.

Our day should be filled with turning to Him, conversing with Him, and also looking for the burning bushes that come across our paths. This is the meaning of Paul's exhortation to the Thessalonians to "pray without ceasing" (1 Thess. 5:17 NKJV).

That said, here are some texts that show us the importance of beginning our mornings with the Lord:

And in the morning, rising up a great while before day, he [Jesus] went out, and departed into a solitary place, and there prayed. (Mark 1:35 KJV)

Meditate in your heart upon your bed, and be still. (Ps. 4:4 NASB)

My voice shalt thou hear in the morning, O LORD; in the morning will I direct my prayer unto thee, and will look up. (Ps. 5:3 KJV)

O God, thou art my God; early will I seek thee: my soul thirsteth for thee, my flesh longeth for thee in a dry and thirsty land, where no water is. (Ps. 63:1 KJV)

> Awake, my soul!
>> Awake, harp and lyre!
>> I will awaken the dawn. (Ps. 57:8)

With my soul have I desired thee in the night; yea, with my spirit within me will I seek thee early. (Isa. 26:9 KJV)

> "The Lord GOD has given Me
> The tongue of the learned,
> That I should know how to speak
> A word in season to him who is weary.
> He awakens Me morning by morning,
> He awakens My ear
> To hear as the learned." (Isa. 50:4 NKJV)

Here are examples of people who rose early to seek the Lord:

- Job (Job 1:5)
- Abraham (Gen. 19:27; 22:3)
- Jacob (Gen. 28:18)
- Moses (Ex. 24:4; 34:4)

- the congregation of Israel (Ex. 16:15–21; Num. 14:40; Judg. 21:4; Hos. 5:15 KJV)
- Joshua (Josh. 6:12; 7:16; 8:10)
- Hannah (1 Sam. 1:19)
- David and Solomon (Pss. 5:3; 57:8; 63:1 KJV; Song 7:12)
- Hezekiah (2 Chron. 29:20)
- Isaiah (Isa. 26:9; 50:4)
- Jeremiah (Jer. 25:3–4 KJV)
- Jesus (Mark 1:35; Luke 21:38; John 8:2)

Our advice: to develop your spiritual senses to discern the Lord's voice, spend time conversing with Him.

Draw near to God and He will draw near to you. (James 4:8 NKJV)

And without faith it is impossible to please God, because anyone who comes to him must believe that he exists and that he rewards those who earnestly seek him. (Heb. 11:6)

Turn to Him in the morning, even if for a brief moment. Our minds tend not to race as much the moment we awaken, so use that moment to turn your heart and mind to Jesus. Take a quiet moment to say a few words to Him; then listen.

Then, as you go about your day, speak to Him, listening, watching, and observing as you engage in your business.

---

*Even so we have felt the Spirit of God operating upon
our hearts, we have known and perceived the power
which he wields over human spirits, and we know
him by frequent, conscious, personal contact.*

—CHARLES SPURGEON[1]

THIRTY

Hearing the Voice While Walking

One of the simplest ways to quiet your soul, turn your attention toward the Lord, and listen to His voice is through a fellowship walk—meaning, fellowship with your Lord as you walk.

The first humans heard the Lord's voice when they walked in the garden.

> Then the man and his wife heard the sound of the LORD God as he was walking in the garden in the cool of the day. (Gen. 3:8)

Since that time, the phrase "walked/walking/walk with God" is used as a metaphor in the Bible for having a close, conversational relationship with the Lord.

> Enoch walked faithfully with God; then he was no more, because God took him away. (Gen. 5:24)

> Noah was a righteous man, blameless among the people of his time, and he walked faithfully with God. (Gen. 6:9)

Believers walk with God, even through the valley of the shadow of death (Ps. 23:4).

A fellowship walk is a very simple exercise: simply put on your shoes and walk outdoors. The key here is to walk slowly. This isn't a power walk.

There are three practices that we encourage you to try as you walk, all of which will help you tune in to the Lord's speaking.

1. As you walk, breathe in and out, remembering that each breath comes from the Lord.

Interestingly, the word for "Spirit" in both Greek and Hebrew is the same word that's translated "breath." So the Holy Spirit is God's Holy Breath.

When God launched the first creation, He breathed His life into the first human being (Gen. 2:7). When God launched the new creation, Jesus—God enfleshed—breathed His life into His disciples (John 20:22).

Breath, then, contains life and signifies life. You can't live without breathing.

Consider these words from the hymn by A. B. Simpson, who understood the significance of breathing while communing with God:

> *O Lord, breathe Thy Spirit on me,*
> *Teach me how to breathe Thee in;*
> *Help me pour into Thy bosom*
> *All my life of self and sin.*
> *I am breathing out my sorrow,*
> *Breathing out my sin;*
> *I am breathing, breathing, breathing,*
> *All Thy fullness in.*
> *I am breathing out my own life,*
> *That I may be filled with Thine;*
> *Letting go my strength and weakness,*
> *Breathing in Thy life divine.*[1]

So walk and concentrate on your breath, the breath of life.

2. As you walk, pour your heart out to the Lord. Share your worries, anxieties, and concerns.

> Trust in him at all times, O people;
>> pour out your heart before him;
>> God is a refuge for us. *Selah.* (Ps. 62:8 ESV)

Very often, while doing this, you will hear the still, calm, loving voice of your Savior, whispering His thoughts, feelings, and impressions through your own thoughts, feelings, and impressions.

3. As you walk, notice God's creation. Observe the trees, the grass, the clouds, the sky, and everything else around you that is from God. According to the apostle Paul, all things were created for Christ, by Christ, and through Christ (Col. 1:16). The visible creation, then, contains the fingerprints of your Lord.

Behold the glory of God in creation as you take your walk.

When you walk and breathe, or walk and pour your heart out, or walk and notice God's creation, you're opening your spirit to the divine whisper.

THIRTY-ONE

Hearing the Voice in Worship

Consider the following three passages where God's people were ministering to the Lord and He spoke to them:

> The boy Samuel ministered before the LORD under Eli. . . . Then Eli realized that the LORD was calling the boy. (1 Sam. 3:1, 8)

> While they were worshiping the Lord and fasting, the Holy Spirit said, "Set apart for me Barnabas and Saul for the work to which I have called them." (Acts 13:2)

> While the harpist was playing, the hand of the LORD came on Elisha. (2 Kings 3:15)

Ministering to the Lord is loving Him through worship songs or spoken praise. It's distinct from supplication (which is praying for your own needs) and intercession (which is praying for others). Ministering to the Lord is loving Him for His own sake.

When we enter a spirit of loving worship through singing or spoken praise, our spirits become more sensitive to hear Jesus speak as well as to receive from Him. In so doing, we turn *off* our souls to the frequencies of the world, turn them *on* to the frequency of the spiritual realm, and tune them *in* to hear the voice of our Lord.

As we explained in *Jesus Manifesto*, Jesus is God's Absolute and Perfect Pitch.[1] As we minister to the Lord, our emotions are reoriented toward Him.

Ministering to the Lord serves as a catalyst that pulls us loose from distractions and allows our hearts to gaze upon His beauty.

THIRTY-TWO

Personalizing the Voice in Scripture

One of the most popular Christian books in recent history is Sarah Young's *Jesus Calling*, a small devotional made up of short chapters wherein Jesus is speaking to the reader. If you look at each chapter closely, however, the sections where Jesus is speaking are drawn straight from Scripture and reworded to have the personalized voice of Christ.

The immense popularity of this book shows us one thing: *God's people are desperate to hear Jesus speak personally to them.*

But the wonderful truth is that you can learn to hear Jesus exactly the same way that author Sarah Young portrays in *Jesus Calling*.

Before we look at some examples of how to personalize the speaking of Jesus in Scripture, you should know that every passage in the Bible is not conducive for the following exercise.

All Scripture can be broken up into two types: passages that are *time-bound* and passages that are *timeless*.

Passages that are time-bound pertain to certain events in history. Passages that are timeless contain spiritual truths that are applicable to us from now until eternity.

For the purposes of illustration, we'll take a few passages from Galatians to distinguish between those that are time-bound and those that are timeless.

Time-Bound Passages

For you have heard of my previous way of life in Judaism, how intensely I persecuted the church of God and tried to destroy it. (Gal. 1:13)

Then after fourteen years, I went up again to Jerusalem, this time with Barnabas. I took Titus along also. (Gal. 2:1)

When Cephas came to Antioch, I opposed him to his face, because he stood condemned. (Gal. 2:11)

These passages are time-bound because they deal with specific events that occurred in the first century. While we can certainly draw important lessons from these events, they are not conducive for personalizing the voice of Jesus in Scripture.

Timeless Passages

Grace and peace to you from God our Father and the Lord Jesus Christ, who gave himself for our sins to rescue us from the present evil age, according to the will of our God and Father, to whom be glory for ever and ever. Amen. (Gal. 1:3–5)

So in Christ Jesus you are all children of God through faith, for all of you who were baptized into Christ have clothed yourselves with Christ. (Gal. 3:26–27)

Because you are his sons, God sent the Spirit of his Son into our hearts, the Spirit who calls out, "Abba, Father." So you are no longer a slave, but God's child; and since you are his child, God has made you also an heir. (Gal. 4:6–7)

These passages contain enduring truths that relate to us now and forever. Timeless passages speak of the character, glory, and love of God. They also speak of what He has done for us in Christ.

Since God the Father is eternal and Jesus Christ is "the same yesterday and today and forever" (Heb. 13:8), such passages are timeless.

Consider that there are only two things on the planet that are God-breathed: the Scriptures and the human spirit.

Then the LORD God formed a man from the dust of the ground and *breathed into his nostrils the breath of life*, and the man became a living being. (Gen. 2:7)

All Scripture is *God-breathed* and is useful for teaching, rebuking, correcting and training in righteousness. (2 Tim. 3:16)

Because you have the Spirit of God residing in you, you can exercise the deepest part of you (your spirit) and hear the living Word of God (Jesus) speak through the written Word of God (the Bible).

This exercise is best done with the Epistles. It can also be done with some sections of the Gospels and the Psalms.

Here's an example from Colossians 1. (This is an excerpt from the afterword of our book *Jesus Manifesto*.) Listen to the voice of Jesus through this passage:

I am the visible image of the invisible God. I existed before anything was created, and I am supreme over all creation, for through Me, My Father created everything in the heavenly realms and on earth.

I made the things you can see and the things you cannot see—such as thrones, kingdoms, rulers, and authorities in the unseen world. Everything was created through Me and for Me.

I existed before anything else, and I hold all creation together.

I am the head of the church, which is My body.

I am the beginning, supreme over all who rise from the dead. So I am first in everything. God in all His fullness was pleased to live in Me, and through Me God reconciled everything to Himself.

I made peace with everything in heaven and on earth by means of My blood on the cross.

This includes you who were once far away from God. You were His enemy, separated from Him by your evil thoughts and actions. Yet now My Father has reconciled you to Himself through My physical death. As a result, He has brought you into His own presence, and you are holy and blameless as you stand before Him without a single fault.

Continue to believe this truth, and stand firmly in it. Don't drift away from the assurance you received when you heard the good news.

This message was kept secret for centuries and generations past, but now it has been revealed to you, for My Father wanted you to know that My riches and glory are for you. And this is the secret: I live in you.[1]

You can use the same exercise by taking several timeless texts, rewording them to be written from the Lord's vantage point, and then tying them together. For example, consider how we used two separate passages from Romans and Ephesians to write this message from Jesus:

My Father has called you according to His eternal purpose—a purpose that He had in His heart from before time. And by His grace, you are part of that purpose. Because of this, everything in your life . . . the good, the bad, and the horrible . . . are working together for your good. Everything that's happened to you has first passed through My hands before it got to you. My Father foreknew you before you were born. And He chose and selected you to be conformed into My image. I am the firstborn among many brothers and sisters, and you are one of them.

If God is for you, who can be against you? It is My Father who has justified you. For He didn't spare me, His only Son, to be delivered for you. How then shall He withhold anything else from you? Who can bring a charge against you? Who is he who can condemn you? I died for you, removing all of your sins, and I rose again from the dead and am now seated at my Father's right hand, making intercession for you.

And My Father has given you all spiritual blessings in the heavenly realms that are all in me. And He chose you in Me before the foundation of the world. Before you took your first breath, you were Mine. According to My Father's good pleasure, you were called to be My sons and daughters, holy and blameless in My love, fully accepted by My Father because you are in Me. And He accepts Me completely. (Based on Romans 8:28–34 and Ephesians 1:3–6)

This is precisely the way that most of *Jesus Calling* is written.

The beautiful thing here is that because you have the Scriptures and a spirit that's indwelt by Jesus Christ, you can have your own "Jesus Calling" experience and hear the Lord speak to you in the same way.

THIRTY-THREE

Sharpening Your Spiritual Instincts

In the natural order of things, the more we exercise something, the better we become at it. The same is true in the spiritual order of things. You can sharpen your spiritual instincts by exercising them regularly:

> But solid food belongs to those who are of full age, that is, those who by
> reason of use have their senses exercised to discern both good and evil.
> (Heb. 5:14 NKJV)

According to the writer of Hebrews, as we exercise our spiritual senses, we become spiritually mature and can consume the strong meat of God's Word.

Our spiritual "senses" are exercised by "reason of use" (or habit) to "discern" both good and evil. In other words, the mature believer is able to discern the will of God in all situations.

So take the practical lessons we've outlined in this book and make them habits. In this way, you will become adept at hearing the voice of your Savior.

PART THREE

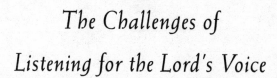

The Challenges of
Listening for the Lord's Voice

THIRTY-FOUR

The Price of Following the Lord's Voice

Sometimes the voice of the Lord will land you in trouble.

Consider this: Jesus lived by His Father's life. He had the mind of His Father, operated by His spiritual instincts, and followed the Father's voice.

Where did the voice of God eventually lead Jesus? *Up a hill to be crucified.*

But it was also the life of the Father who raised Jesus from the dead. (Perhaps the Father said to Jesus, "Come forth," just as Jesus said to Lazarus.)

Recall that what the Father was to Jesus, Jesus Christ is to all of us. So where will the voice of Jesus lead you? To lay your life down. To take up your cross. To die to your self. But the life of Jesus will also raise you from the dead.

> We always carry around in our body the death of Jesus, so that the life of Jesus may also be revealed in our body. For we who are alive are always being given over to death for Jesus' sake, so that his life may also be revealed in our mortal body. So then, death is at work in us, but life is at work in you. (2 Cor. 4:10–12)

Indeed, there is a danger in following the voice of your Lord. It very well may land you in trouble. Some of the greatest saints in history paid a high price for following the voice of Jesus.

It got Paul of Tarsus beheaded.

It got Peter crucified.

It got John Huss burned alive.

It got William Tyndale strangled.

It caused John Wesley to be slandered mercilessly.

Why?

Because each of these men followed the voice of his Lord and it caused him to challenge the status quo.

Yet for all who lay their lives down, there's always a resurrection.

THIRTY-FIVE

The Challenge of Our Expectations

One of the main reasons we've written this book is to give you practical handles on how to recognize the Lord's voice.

That said, there are some dangers related to hearing and following the Lord's voice. One of them is the idea that Jesus will always speak to you in the same manner.

Before Jesus entered into the human drama, the nation of Israel was waiting for a political Messiah to deliver them from their enemies. However, the way that Jesus, God's Messiah, arrived on the planet was completely unexpected.

When Jesus grew up, the religious leaders didn't recognize Him as the Messiah, even though He ate, drank, and taught in their midst (Luke 13:26). What's more striking is that the disciples didn't even recognize who Jesus was most of the time, because He continued to break out of their expectations.

This is one of the reasons why He said, "Blessed is he who is not offended because of Me" (Matt. 11:6 NKJV). Jesus said this in regard to John the Baptist, because Jesus wasn't meeting John's expectations.

But Jesus is the same today, yesterday, and forever. Hence, He still refuses to meet all of our expectations. (Unfortunately, some people become offended with Him because of this.[1])

Indeed, the Lord delights in expanding your view of Him. He enjoys showing Himself to be larger than your expectations. Sometimes He will speak to you through people and groups that you may be inclined to write off and reject. Sometimes He will speak to you through an article or a book you are inclined to ignore.

You may think to yourself, *But their doctrine is off. Their theology is messed up. They are too legalistic. They are too libertine. Surely, Jesus can't speak to me through them.*

Really?

Yes, they are imperfect. For sure. *Just like you are.*

This is why humility and openness to His voice—through any person or group—is critical. And it requires deep humility.

Here's a lesson to learn: *the Lord Jesus Christ eventually comes to us in ways that make it easy for us to reject Him.*

We've watched this scenario play out repeatedly among Christians who were part of movements, coalitions, and denominations that felt they were holding to the pure orthodox teachings of the Bible. This made them apt to turn a deaf ear to the other parts of the body of Christ.

But the Lord Jesus doesn't dance to our music. He doesn't sing to our tune.

A true mark of spiritual poverty is a wide heart. If you have a narrow heart, you will only recognize Jesus through *some* of His people.

What, then, does our Lord do when we fail to receive Him when He comes to us in an unexpected way?

He moves on. And we cease to grow.

The danger of having our lampstands removed still exists (Rev. 2:5).

Jesus is full of surprises. We can't nail Him down into our theological systems or doctrinal boxes. He will always break out.

Like Mary Magdalene, we have a tendency to cling to the Jesus with whom we are familiar. And this sometimes means we end up turning the real Christ away unwittingly.

When Jesus was transfigured before Peter, James, and John, Peter wanted to build a special dwelling place for Jesus, Moses, and Elijah and remain on the mountain to enjoy the holy sight. But God interrupted Peter in midstream, for He would not allow it (Matt. 17:1–13).

Like Peter, we are tempted to want to build a monument around a spiritual experience with Jesus and remain there. But God will not have it. He will break free from our frail attempts to hold Him down. And He does so by coming to us in new and unexpected ways.

Jesus Christ is vaster than what most of us think, and He works through a lot more people than we would expect.

In sum, if Jesus isn't surprising you, you've probably stopped growing spiritually. Following Him wherever He goes and however He comes is God's way of keeping us humble and open, like a child.

THIRTY-SIX

The Danger of Arrogance

If you've learned nothing else from this book, we hope you've learned this: God made you His child, so you are important enough to Him for Jesus to speak to you personally. But you're not so important that hearing the Lord's voice makes you special. Hearing Jesus is the privilege of *all* His followers.

All who are led by the Spirit of God are children of God. (Rom. 8:14 NLT)

Sometimes, hearing the voice of the Lord and gaining insights into the things of God can make a person proud and arrogant.

Paul's famous "thorn in the flesh" was given to him as a safeguard to keep him from being puffed up with pride because of the dramatic revelations he received from the Lord.

And lest I should be exalted above measure by the abundance of the revelations, a thorn in the flesh was given to me, a messenger of Satan to buffet me, lest I be exalted above measure. (2 Cor. 12:7 NKJV)

This text gives us insight into a common tendency that occurs when we receive something special from the Lord. The danger is to think that we are more special than other believers.

With every new insight into the Lord, there is the temptation to become proud. There seems to be a subtle arrogance that seeks to seep into the human heart when one experiences a deeper experience or understanding of Christ.

But there is nothing more opposite of the Spirit of Jesus Christ than the spirit of pride and arrogance.

A famous saying goes like this: It's possible to be "pure as angels and as proud as devils." We disagree. If you're proud, you're not pure. For God resists the proud (James 4:6 NKJV; 1 Peter 5:5 NKJV).

As we said in the beginning, we find Jesus in a spirit of poverty. A spirit of poverty says, "I need to know Him more. I don't have the corner on Him. I am a child in this business. I'm still in school. I'm still learning. I haven't arrived."

How well can you know Jesus?

You can know Him in proportion to the poverty that's in your heart. "Blessed are the poor in spirit," Jesus said (Matt. 5:3). The opposite of that statement is what the Laodicean church said of herself: "I am rich, have become wealthy, and have need of nothing" (Rev. 3:17 NKJV).

Here's a prayer worth praying. Whenever you learn something new about the Lord that steals your breath, that's the time to turn to Him and say, "Lord, let me not lose touch. Keep my feet on the ground and cause me to always remember that I am no better than any other Christian." For it is in times of great revelation that we need the humility of Christ the most.

Consider the church in Ephesus. Paul lived in Ephesus for three years raising up a church. By his own testimony, he proclaimed "the whole counsel of God" to the believers there (Acts 20:27 NKJV).

Paul unveiled to the Ephesian believers the matchless vision of the eternal purpose of God. He spoke to them about the mystery of the ages in great depths (Eph. 1–3; 6:19; Col. 1–2; 4:3).

Paul held meetings in a space called the school of Tyrannus, where he declared Christ and trained young workers. Timothy, Titus, and six other men were present as his apprentices. Those young apprentices probably ministered to the Ephesian church as well.

After Paul was imprisoned, Timothy moved to Ephesus and ministered to the church there for a number of years. Some years later, the beloved disciple, John, ended up in Ephesus. Apollos, who was "mighty in the Scriptures," also spent time in Ephesus (Acts 18:24 NASB); perhaps the Ephesian church benefited from his ministry as well.

The church in Ephesus received the deepest and highest revelation of Christ through choice servants of God, including Paul, John, Timothy, Titus, and Apollos. But as the New Testament closes, we learn that the church in Ephesus was rebuked by Jesus for having left its first love (Rev. 2:1–4).

What happened? They probably stopped pursuing Him. They became fat, content, and proud. They clung to the Jesus they were given so richly and stopped moving forward. They became proud and arrogant because of the great insights they had been given about Christ.

Let this story serve as a cautionary tale. May we never allow pride to close our ears to the voice of the Savior.

THIRTY-SEVEN

The Danger of Counterfeit Voices

It's been said that wherever God is working, the devil sets up shop nearby.[1]

When God is operating powerfully in a person or group, counterfeit spiritual manifestations will sometimes surface in the group or through people attacking the person or group whom God is using. This has been true historically.

For example, the Welsh Revival of the early twentieth century is one of a number of authentic moves of God that was destroyed because people started to accept counterfeit spiritual manifestations.[2]

How do you know when Jesus, through the Holy Spirit, is speaking to you directly or through someone else?

The Scriptures exhort us to judge in such matters:

Let two or three prophets speak, and let the others pass judgment. (1 Cor. 14:29 NASB)

Do not despise prophetic utterances. But examine everything carefully; hold fast to that which is good; abstain from every form of evil. (1 Thess. 5:20–22 NASB)

"Do not judge according to appearance, but judge with righteous judgment." (John 7:24 NASB)

And this I pray, that your love may abound still more and more in real knowledge and all discernment. (Phil. 1:9 NASB)

Here are some guidelines to know the true from the counterfeit. When the message is from the Holy Spirit . . .

- It points people to Jesus. It glorifies and lifts up Christ. It puts the spotlight on Jesus and causes people to be more excited about Him. The fruit is that they want to follow and love Him more.
- It brings unity and a sense of oneness among true Jesus followers.
- It causes love for the brethren to rise up and be awakened in the hearts of God's people.
- It may cause true conviction and repentance if there is a present sin happening (repentance means to stop the sin).
- The person who is walking in the Spirit doesn't go on the offensive if he or she is attacked. (See my blog post "Jesus and Paul Under Fire" for examples.)[3]

When a message is not from the Holy Spirit, but is a counterfeit . . .

- It will invariably end up producing division and discord among God's people. As Proverbs says, "Things the LORD hates . . . A false witness who speaks lies, and one who sows discord among brethren" (Prov. 6:16, 19 NKJV). Unfortunately, some Christians lack the discernment to recognize when seeds of discord are being sown right in front of them. Dividing a body of believers is like taking a butcher knife to Jesus Christ and cutting Him up into pieces. *It's very serious.* Paul gives us this image in 1 Corinthians 1:10–13.
- It produces confusion, and God is not the author of confusion (1 Cor. 14:33 NKJV).
- It is pushy and condemning. (By contrast, God's voice draws and encourages.)

- It is often associated with gossip and slander. As we have already shared, the word *devil* means "slanderer." Scripture calls him "the accuser of [the] brethren" (Rev. 12:10 NKJV), which is a description of his nature. Slandering or accusing a person of things you subjectively "sense" or "feel," without hard evidence to support it, is sinful. The gift of discerning spirits and the word of knowledge are *not the same* as judging someone's motives and shouldn't be confused with it. The latter is sin. Gossip is especially dangerous when cloaked with spiritual language, such as, "The Lord showed me thus and such about Sally." According to Proverbs, gossip destroys trust and "separates close friends" (Prov. 16:28). This is one of the reasons why God hates it so much.
- It doesn't put Christ in the spotlight; rather, it puts a person or a person's alleged gift in the spotlight. People who lift themselves up while tearing others down are not operating in a true spiritual gift. They are in the flesh and are operating in a counterfeit.
- It's not easily entreated, but comes through in a dominating, overconfident, and strong-willed manner. It cannot be questioned or challenged. The person using the "gift" cannot hear correction, even from multiple and credible voices.
- It's usually motivated by jealousy of others and the desire to be recognized and honored. James made this quite clear.

In James 3:13–18, James gives us the criteria by which to judge whether God is speaking or not.

If it's God who is speaking ("the wisdom from above"), it has these marks upon it:

- It is gentle.
- It is open to reason.
- It is considerate.
- It is willing to yield.
- It is pure.

- It is full of mercy.
- It bears good fruit.
- It is unwavering.
- It is void of hypocrisy.

When a source other than God is speaking ("the wisdom that doesn't come from above"), it contains these marks:

- It is sensual (unspiritual).
- It is fleshly (earthly).
- It is demonic.
- It produces discord.
- It produces confusion.
- It produces disorder and other evil things.

According to James, if a person's heart is full of jealousy and selfish ambition, he or she will be susceptible to confusing God's wisdom with "demonic" wisdom. In the next chapter, James goes on to say:

Do not speak against one another, brethren. He who speaks against a brother or judges his brother, speaks against the law and judges the law; but if you judge the law, you are not a doer of the law but a judge of it. (James 4:11 NASB)

Know this: the state of your heart will determine if you are susceptible to confusing the Lord's voice with a counterfeit.

For this reason, the writer of Hebrews warned his readers to not harden their hearts when the Lord speaks to them:

"Today, if you hear his voice,
      do not harden your hearts." (Heb. 3:15)

Some of the prophets in the Old Testament confused the Lord's voice with a counterfeit voice due to the state of their hearts. In Jeremiah 23, we learn that some prophets spoke a vision that originated from their own minds (v. 16). Because of their evil deeds, these prophets couldn't distinguish between the Lord's voice and the deceit of their own hearts (vv. 22, 26).

In like manner, the Corinthians couldn't discern the Holy Spirit's voice from the voice of their own flesh because they were living carnally. So they confused the two (1 Cor. 2–3). Therefore, the best antidote to preventing deception is to make sure your heart is being nurtured by the principles outlined in part 1. If you are living in the flesh, you will confuse the Lord's voice with the desires of your fallen nature.

Tragically, projecting onto God what's in our own hearts is quite common today:

> To the faithful you show yourself faithful,
>> to the blameless you show yourself blameless,
> to the pure you show yourself pure,
>> but to the devious you show yourself shrewd. (Ps. 18:25–26)

I've seen this happen many times. Throughout the years, I've met people who swore that "God told them" to do all sorts of self-indulgent things.

Such deception is real and should be understood.[4]

THIRTY-EIGHT

The Danger of Forcing
a Word from God

In *The Message* translation, Romans 12:6 says, "Let's just go ahead and be what we were made to be, without enviously or pridefully comparing ourselves with each other, or trying to be something we aren't."

It's not uncommon for Christians who keep hearing their friends say, "The Lord said to me such and such," to feel the pressure of getting a word from God so they, too, can say, "The Lord told me . . ."

This pressure is where a great deal of fakery and deception lies. In their desperation, countless Christians will grab hold of anything and call it the Lord's speaking.

The game of "Bible roulette," where a person flips through the Bible and sticks his finger in it, superstitiously taking whatever text he's pointing at to be God's personal word for him, is one example. This practice is not dissimilar to King Saul's profound mistake of consulting a witch to get direction from God (1 Sam. 28 THE MESSAGE).

The Bible wasn't written to play with like a Ouija board. It's meant to be understood within its own context.

Be assured that the Lord *does* speak to you. Psalm 32:8 promises us, "I will instruct you and teach you in the way you should go; I will counsel you with my loving eye on you." But the truth is that many Christians exaggerate both the way and the frequency of God's speaking to them. So never let someone's hyper-spiritual testimonials discourage you or make you feel inferior.

THIRTY-NINE

The Danger of Misunderstanding

It's possible to hear the Lord correctly but misinterpret what He's saying to us. Even the Lord's own disciples experienced this difficulty when He was on earth.

Jesus made a statement about how Peter would die. Peter then asked Jesus how John would die. The Lord's response was simple: "If I want him to remain alive until I return, what is that to you? You must follow me" (John 21:22).

The disciples misunderstood what the Lord said and started a rumor based on their faulty interpretation of His words.

John recorded the incident, saying, "Then this saying went out among the brethren that this disciple [John] would not die. Yet Jesus did not say to him that he would not die, but, 'If I will that he remain till I come, what is that to you?'" (John 21:23 NKJV).

The same happens today. We may hear the Lord speak to us, but that doesn't mean we have interpreted what He's said correctly. We can unintentionally distort it. The perfection of the speaker (Jesus) doesn't guarantee the perfection of the hearer.

Consequently, one must seek to *understand* what the Lord says, especially before acting on or repeating it to others.

As we've already pointed out, the Lord in His mercy often speaks to us in unclear ways to allow us the space and time to respond or to seek Him for more understanding. This forces us to grow into His mind, which is so different from ours (Isa. 55:8).

So the Lord's voice sometimes causes us to struggle to understand, forcing us to exclaim with the psalmist in frustration:

> Oh, that You would rend the heavens!
> That You would come down!
> That the mountains might shake at Your presence. (Isa. 64:1 NKJV)

During such times, the Lord is wanting us to patiently seek Him for wisdom, to get counsel from those who are spiritually mature, and to never move in haste.

All those biblical texts about waiting on the Lord and seeking His face come into play when we strive to avoid misinterpreting the voice of the Lord.

> But those who wait on the LORD
> Shall renew their strength;
> They shall mount up with wings like eagles,
> They shall run and not be weary,
> They shall walk and not faint. (Isa. 40:31 NKJV)

> I would have lost heart, unless I had believed
> That I would see the goodness of the LORD
> In the land of the living.
> Wait on the LORD;
> Be of good courage,
> And He shall strengthen your heart;
> Wait, I say, on the LORD! (Ps. 27:13–14 NKJV)

> The LORD is good to those who wait for Him,
> To the soul who seeks Him. (Lam. 3:25 NKJV)

I wait for the LORD, my soul waits,

And in His word I do hope.

My soul waits for the LORD

More than those who watch for the morning—

Yes, more than those who watch for the morning. (Ps. 130:5–6 NKJV;

    see also Pss. 27:14; 37:7)

Another reason why we can misunderstand what the Lord is saying to us has to do with our conversational styles and our natural dispositions. As I pointed out in my book *Revise Us Again*, people who are inclined toward intellectualism tend to recognize a word from the Lord only when it's couched in biblical references and theological arguments. People who are inclined toward emotionalism tend to recognize a word from the Lord only when it's couched in "thus says the Lord" or other prophetic statements. And people who are inclined toward action (volition) tend to recognize a word from the Lord only when it involves some kind of activity.[1]

To simplify the point, thinkers, feelers, and doers tend to recognize the Lord's speaking only when it resembles their specific personalities and communication styles. For this reason, we must learn to hear Jesus speak to us outside of our comfort zones and personal preferences.

FORTY

The Danger of Misrepresenting God

Some people speak as though God is talking to them every second. If a twig moves or they see an image in the clouds, "God showed" them something.

The danger here is that, beyond the exaggerated claims that typically go with such statements, we don't find support for this anywhere in the New Testament.

As I've explored in my book *Revise Us Again*, the phrases "God told me" and "The Lord told me" are classic Christianese.[1]

Very often, when people use phrases like these, it's for one of the following reasons:

1. The person wants to do something and wants to avoid criticism from others. Who can argue with "God told me to do it"?
2. The person *doesn't* want to do something and wants to stop being bothered about it. Who can argue with "The Lord told me not to"?
3. The person wants to appear spiritual in the eyes of others.
4. The person wants to evade responsibility for the action, putting it on God. We've both seen people do outrageous things, claiming "God told me to do it." Sigh.

5. Many people use this phrase simply out of peer pressure. It's the way the Christians they associate with talk, so they adopt the Christianeze themselves.

6. Sometimes people will use the "The Lord told me to tell you . . ." phrase out of unresolved anger or jealousy.

All of these examples are abuses and misuses of the Lord's voice.

There are several reasons why banishing "God told me" from your vocabulary is a good idea:

1. We never see the New Testament authors talking this way. (While they sometimes prophesy, we don't see them pulling the "God told me" card.)

2. It makes other people feel inferior if they don't feel God is speaking to them the way He speaks to you.

If God didn't truly tell you what you think He did—even if you believe He did—you are misrepresenting the Lord.

Unfortunately, the Lord routinely gets credit for things He never authored and blamed for things He never thought up. *You don't want to add to this problem.*

When Paul was forced to share his deep spiritual experiences, he admitted that he was playing the fool by doing so (2 Cor. 12:1ff.).

When we read Paul's letters to the churches—as well as those of Peter, James, John, and the rest—we never read them saying, "God told me." Instead, they simply write what they believe to be the Lord's will without wrapping it in the "God told me to say this" package.

The very worst is saying to someone, "God told me to tell you . . ." True prophetic words do not need to be prefaced that way.

And very often, when the Lord reveals something to you about someone else, it's not so you can go to that person and say, "Jesus told me this about you." Instead, it's so you can intercede for him or her. Or so you can gain insight on how to more effectively minister to that person.

As Oswald Chambers once put it, "God never gives us discernment in order that we may criticize, but that we may intercede."[2]

Our advice: when Jesus speaks to you, just follow what He says. There's no need to wave a big flag over it with slogans like "The Lord told me."

FORTY-ONE

The Danger of Religious Jealousy

When God chose to speak to Moses, his two siblings—Aaron and Miriam—became jealous.

> Then Miriam and Aaron spoke against Moses because of the Ethiopian woman whom he had married; for he had married an Ethiopian woman. So they said, "Has the LORD indeed spoken only through Moses? Has He not spoken through us also?" And the LORD heard it. (Now the man Moses was very humble, more than all men who were on the face of the earth.) (Num. 12:1–3 NKJV)

Even though the voice of the Lord is the heritage of all of God's children, some of them will become jealous of you just because your ears are more attuned to Jesus than theirs. This is a serious danger, because the repercussions of religious jealousy are enormous.

Abel lost his life because his brother Cain was jealous of his relationship with God.

King Saul became jealous because of the favor of God in David's life. That jealousy moved him to try to kill David.

Jesus was put to death by those who were envious of His life and ministry (Matt. 27:18 NKJV; Mark 15:10 NKJV). That jealousy seems to have taken root when Jesus was drawing larger crowds than both John the Baptist and the Pharisees:

> The Pharisees had heard that [Jesus] was gaining and baptizing more disciples than John. . . . So he left Judea and went back once more to Galilee. (John 4:1, 3)

The servant is not greater than his master. If the Lord begins leading you, there will be spiritual fruit in your life evident for others to see. And as a result, others will become jealous of you.

People who are jealous become obsessed with tearing the objects of their jealousy down, misrepresenting them, distorting their words, and maligning them—all while lifting themselves up in the process. It's a pattern that's woven into the flesh.

However, your reaction is everything. If you respond in kind, you will lose the Lord's favor. But if you choose the path of David and Jesus, entrusting it to God and not returning evil for evil, the Lord's favor will only increase in your life and He will produce more fruit through your ministry. The Lord stands with those who refuse to retaliate but are willing to leave the matter in His hands.

The words of Peter say it all: "When they hurled their insults at him, he did not retaliate; when he suffered, he made no threats. Instead, he entrusted himself to him who judges justly" (1 Peter 2:23).

FORTY-TWO

The Danger of Misinterpreting
Dry Spells and Dark Nights

The spiritual walk passes through seasons. In fact, the seasons in nature teach us about the seasons in the spiritual life.

There are wet spells and downpours (revivals). There is the growth of spring (spiritual progress). Then there are the cold winters (trials). In addition, there are dry spells and dark nights.

Dry spells are normal in the Christian walk. They don't indicate that there is sin or rebellion in your life. Rather, the Lord weans us through them, taking us to another level of spiritual growth as it concerns our motives for following Him.

Among other things, dry spells teach us whether or not we are following Jesus Christ or Santa Claus. Meaning, are we serving Him *for Him* or for His blessings? Dry spells weed many Christians out in this regard.

The dark night, however, is something more severe and far less common.

A well-known Christian in the sixteenth century coined the term *the dark night of the soul*. The term refers to an experience when God removes the "sense" of His presence from a believer's life.

We realize that talking about "the sense" of God's presence may lead you to believe we're escorting you into Spooksville. But stay with us.

Many Christians respond to this kind of language by saying, "But I'm not sure that I ever sense God's presence to begin with."

If you truly are born from above, you actually have a sense of God's presence at all times.

Why? Because the Lord lives inside of you. If His presence were removed, you would notice immediately. For example, a fish doesn't "sense" the water it lives in because it's always in it. But if the fish were removed from the water, the fish would instantly know.

The presence of God in the believer's life is the same way. Like a wedding ring, it can often be overlooked because it's always there.

Granted, if you give specific attention to the Lord—through prayer, praise, worship, and otherwise—you are made *aware* of His presence. But the sense of His presence is always "on" in the background of your consciousness.

That said, the dark night is the experience when God seemingly walks off the stage of your life. If it were to happen to you, you would immediately notice that the sense of His presence had been taken away from you. It's the fish being removed from its water.

In this state, you neither hear nor sense God. Even though you still believe in Him, you *feel* like an atheist.

This rare experience is not a dry spell. Nor is it a punishment or chastisement. In fact, it has nothing to do with one's conduct.

Some of the godliest Christians—past and present—have experienced the dark night.

In such cases, God is teaching His beloved how to know Him apart from feelings, senses, impressions, or anything else.

The dark night, then, is a path to greater spiritual maturity.

I've discussed this experience in much more detail in *Revise Us Again*.[1] But in this book, we wanted to alert you to it with a few practical tips. If you ever have the displeasure of this rare experience, keep these three things in mind:

1. The Lord has promised to always be with you and never leave you (Matt. 28:20; Heb. 13:5). The *sense* of His presence is not the same as the *reality* of His presence, which is always with you.
2. The Lord is ultimately behind the experience. His purpose in it is redemptive and constructive (Ps. 139:12; Rom. 8:28).
3. Do not be alarmed. Keep following the Lord "in the dark" and trust Him in the midst of it. He will bring forth hidden riches out of the darkness.

> And I will give you treasures hidden in the darkness—
>   secret riches.
> I will do this so you may know that I am the LORD,
>   the God of Israel, the one who calls you by name. (Isa. 45:3 NLT)

FORTY-THREE

The Goal of It All

Archbishop William Temple once said, "We only know what Man is when God dwells in him."[1] Indeed, it takes God to be human.

God's desire in creating humans was to impart His life into them so they could make Him visible in the earth and exercise His authority. That's what the Tree of Life was all about.

Jesus Christ is the Tree of Life incarnate. Those who partake of Him shall live by Him (John 6:57 KJV). This is the meaning of Paul's words, "It is no longer I who live, but Christ lives in me" (Gal. 2:20 NKJV).

In this book, we've sought to give you practical advice on how to hear the Lord's voice for yourself. Yet it's important to realize that the primary goal for a Jesus follower is not simply to hear the voice of Jesus and follow it.

It's to know the One who speaks and to be shaped by His voice.

God's goal is to conform you into the image of His Son (Rom. 8:28–29). His ultimate intention is to bring "many sons and daughters to glory" (Heb. 2:10). God's glory is the highest expression of His life.[2]

Understanding God's grand goal—or His eternal purpose—helps us discern the Lord's voice in our daily lives, because everything He does is working toward the fulfillment of that grand and glorious purpose or will (Eph. 1:11).

There is only one will that stands behind the universe. God's eternal purpose is His all-governing will.

In him we were also chosen, having been predestined according to the plan of him who works out everything in conformity with the purpose of his will. (Eph. 1:11)

Therefore do not be foolish, but understand what the Lord's will is. (Eph. 5:17)

Many Christians today want God to instruct and command them. But God is after a mind.

Let this mind be in you which was also in Christ Jesus. (Phil. 2:5 NKJV)

We have the mind of Christ. (1 Cor. 2:16)

We are the sons and daughters of God, who possess minds of our own, rather than just servants who merely take orders (John 15:15; Gal. 4:1ff.).

Jesus, as the Son of Man, had the mind of His Father. And we have been given access to the mind of Christ.

When we walk in the steps of Jesus, which is to live fully for God's will (or eternal purpose), making it the controlling factor in our lives, then we begin to discern the Lord's mind more clearly.

"For I have come down from heaven not to do my will but to do the will of him who sent me." (John 6:38)

And he died for all, that those who live should no longer live for themselves but for him who died for them and was raised again. (2 Cor. 5:15)

Again, having a consciousness—or a mind—is more than hearing a set of commands. Having the Lord's mind means that we understand something of what He thinks, how He feels, and what He desires.

At bottom, the Lord is interested in a relationship with you. He doesn't want to command you like a robot. He wants you to know Him so well that you already know how He thinks and feels. In fact, He wants you to anticipate what He desires.

We are the Lord's friends (John 15:13–15), His fellow workers (1 Cor. 3:9 NKJV), members of His own body (1 Cor. 12:27ff.), and parts of His beloved bride (2 Cor. 11:2; Eph. 5:25–32).

Knowing the Lord, then, is the most important thing in life.

> But whatever were gains to me I now consider loss for the sake of Christ. What is more, I consider everything a loss because of the surpassing worth of knowing Christ Jesus my Lord, for whose sake I have lost all things. I consider them garbage, that I may gain Christ. (Phil. 3:7–8)

Unfortunately, many Christians today who are busy serving Jesus, studying the Bible, and even praying don't know the Lord very well:

> Jesus said to him, "Have I been with you so long, and you still do not know me, Philip?" (John 14:9 ESV)

Knowing the Lord began with your new birth into Christ, when you received eternal life:

> And this is eternal life, that they may know You, the only true God, and Jesus Christ whom You have sent. (John 17:3 NKJV)

Knowing the Lord is the promise of the new covenant.

> "This is the covenant I will establish with the people of Israel
> after that time, declares the Lord.

I will put my laws in their minds
  and write them on their hearts.
I will be their God,
  and they will be my people.
No longer will they teach their neighbor,
  or say to one another, 'Know the Lord,'
because they will all know me,
  from the least of them to the greatest.
For I will forgive their wickedness
  and will remember their sins no more." (Heb. 8:10–12)

Knowing the Lord was the chief pursuit of one of the greatest Christians who ever lived, Paul of Tarsus: "That I may know Him . . ." (Phil. 3:10 NKJV).

In short, the goal of hearing the Lord's voice in our lives is to be shaped by that voice so that we may know the Lord better, love Him more, and be more like Him.

This, of course, will bleed into our service for Him.

Someone may be wondering, "But 1 John 2:27 says we don't need any man to teach us, so why do we need any instruction on how to hear the Lord's voice?" But the Bible also says that God has placed teachers in His church (1 Cor. 12:28; Eph. 4:11). These texts aren't in conflict.

When it comes to hearing the Lord's voice, at first, we need to be given some instruction on how to recognize His voice (hence this book). But afterward, we need no such assistance, because the ability comes with experience.

All of this, then, is the goal of hearing the Lord's voice. Paul's prayer for the Colossian Christians sums it up nicely:

So we have not stopped praying for you since we first heard about you. We ask God to give you complete knowledge of his will and to give you spiritual wisdom and understanding. Then the way you live will always honor and please the Lord, and your lives will produce every kind of good fruit. All the while, you will grow as you learn to know God better and better. We also pray that you will be strengthened with all his glorious power so you will have all the endurance and patience you need. (Col. 1:9–11 NLT)

Jesus, your Lord, is knocking at the door of your heart, longing to commune with you. We hope that this book equips you to open that door.

"This is my Son, whom I love. . . . Listen to him!"
—MATTHEW 17:5

Jesus Speaks After His Ascension

According to John 1:1, Jesus is the *logos*, or Word. This means that Jesus is God's speech and utterance. When God speaks under the new covenant today, He speaks in and through Jesus, the Living Word (Heb. 1:1–2).

In a sentence, Jesus is what God has to say.

With that in mind, the following list contains the times when Jesus spoke to His followers after His ascension.

Getting familiar with Christ's postresurrection speaking (the first section of this book) as well as with His post-ascension speaking (this chapter) will help us become familiar with how Jesus speaks to us today.

In Acts 1:2, Luke said that until the day Jesus was taken up to heaven, He gave instructions through the Holy Spirit to His chosen apostles. Luke teaches us here that the resurrected Christ speaks through the Holy Spirit. Consequently, cases where Jesus speaks through the Spirit— also called "the Spirit of Jesus" (Acts 16:7), "the Spirit of Jesus Christ" (Phil. 1:19), and "the Spirit of Christ" (Rom. 8:9; 1 Peter 1:11)—are also included in this list.

Acts 1:4–8: Jesus told His disciples not to leave Jerusalem, but to wait for the promise of the Father, who would baptize them in the Holy Spirit. He told them that it was not for them to know the times and dates that the Father has set by His own authority and that they would receive power when the Holy Spirit comes on them, making them His witnesses from Jerusalem to the ends of the earth. It is here that Jesus ascended into heaven.

Acts 8:29: The Spirit of Jesus told Philip to join a chariot in which an Ethiopian eunuch was riding.

Acts 9:3–6: Jesus asked Saul why he was persecuting Him. Jesus revealed Himself to be the One whom Saul was persecuting and told him to go into the city to wait for further instructions (see also Acts 22:7–10).

In Acts 26:14–18, the same story reads this way:

"I heard a voice saying to me in Aramaic, 'Saul, Saul, why do you persecute me? It is hard for you to kick against the goads.'

"Then I asked, 'Who are you, Lord?'

"'I am Jesus, whom you are persecuting,' the Lord replied. 'Now get up and stand on your feet. I have appeared to you to appoint you as a servant and as a witness of what you have seen and will see of me. I will rescue you from your own people and from the Gentiles. I am sending you to them to open their eyes and turn them from darkness to light, and from the power of Satan to God, so that they may receive forgiveness of sins and a place among those who are sanctified by faith in me.'"

Acts 9:10–16: Jesus appeared to Ananias in a vision, calling his name. He told Ananias to go to a specific house and ask for Saul. He told Ananias that He had called Saul to proclaim His name to the Gentiles, to kings, and to the people of Israel. He also let Ananias know that He would show Saul the things he would suffer for His name.

Acts 10:19–20: The Spirit of Jesus told Peter to greet three men who were looking for him. The Spirit instructed Peter to go with the men without doubting (see also Acts 11:12).

Acts 11:28: The Spirit of Jesus showed Agabus that a famine was coming.

Acts 13:2: The Spirit of Jesus spoke in the midst of a prayer meeting, saying to set apart Barnabas and Saul for the Lord's work.

Acts 15:28: The apostles made a decision with the guidance of the Spirit.

Acts 16:6: The Spirit of Jesus forbade Paul and his company to travel into Asia to preach the gospel.

Acts 16:7: The Spirit of Jesus prevented Paul and his company from traveling into Bithynia.

Acts 18:9–10: Jesus appeared to Paul in a vision, saying, "Do not be afraid, but speak, and do not keep silent; for I am with you, and no one will attack you to hurt you; for I have many people in this city" (NKJV).

Acts 20:23: The Spirit testified in many cities that chains and tribulations awaited Paul.

Acts 21:11: The Spirit of Jesus spoke through Agabus, saying that Paul would be bound in Jerusalem by the Jews and delivered into the hands of the Gentiles.

Acts 22:17–21: After Paul's conversion, Jesus revealed Himself to Paul while he was in the temple, saying that he must get out of Jerusalem quickly because the people would not receive his testimony there. After Paul responded to Jesus, the Lord told him to depart, for He was going to send him far away from Jerusalem to the Gentiles.

Acts 23:11: While Paul was in jail in Jerusalem, Jesus said to him, "Be of good cheer, Paul; for as you have testified for Me in Jerusalem, so you must also bear witness at Rome" (NKJV).

2 Corinthians 12:7–9: Paul asked the Lord to remove a "thorn in the flesh" from his life. Jesus responded to him, saying, "My grace is sufficient for you, for My strength is made perfect in weakness" (NKJV).

Galatians 4:6: Paul said that the Spirit of Christ cries in our hearts, saying, "Abba, Father."

2 Peter 1:13–14: Peter said that Jesus had made clear to him that he would soon lay aside his earthly body.

Revelation 1:10–16: Jesus told John to write on a scroll what he saw and send it to seven churches in Asia Minor.

Revelation 1:17–18: Jesus told John not to be afraid, that He is the First and the Last, the Living One, the one who was dead and is alive forever, and who holds the keys of death and hades.

Revelation 1:19–3:22: Jesus gave a specific message to seven churches in Asia Minor.

Revelation 14:13: John heard a voice from heaven saying, "Write this: Blessed are the dead who die in the Lord from now on." Then the Spirit of Jesus said, "Yes . . . they will rest from their labor, for their deeds will follow them."

Revelation 16:15: Jesus said, "Look, I come like a thief! Blessed is the one who stays awake and remains clothed, so as not to go naked and be shamefully exposed."

Revelation 21:5–8: Jesus said:

"Behold, I make all things new. . . . Write, for these words are true and faithful. . . . It is done! I am the Alpha and the Omega, the Beginning and the End. I will give of the fountain of the water of life freely to him who thirsts. He who overcomes shall inherit all things, and I will be his God and he shall be My son. But the cowardly, unbelieving, abominable, murderers, sexually immoral, sorcerers, idolaters, and all liars shall have their part in the lake which burns with fire and brimstone, which is the second death." (NKJV)

Revelation 22:7: Jesus announced, "Behold, I am coming quickly! Blessed is he who keeps the words of the prophecy of this book" (NKJV).

Revelation 22:12–20: Jesus said:

"'And behold, I am coming quickly, and My reward is with Me, to give to every one according to his work. I am the Alpha and the Omega, the Beginning and the End, the First and the Last. . . . I, Jesus, have sent My angel to testify to you these things in the churches. I am the Root and the Offspring of David, the Bright and Morning Star.' And the Spirit and the bride say, 'Come!' And let him who hears say, 'Come!' And let him who thirsts come. Whoever desires, let him take the water of life freely. . . . 'Surely I am coming quickly.'" (NKJV)

In the above texts, we see Jesus revealing, confirming, directing, warning, predicting, comforting, and encouraging His followers. The list illustrates the different kinds of things Jesus says and reveals when He speaks to His disciples today, for He is the same today as He was then (Heb. 13:8).

To add a further thought, Jesus said the Holy Spirit would do the following things after He ascended to the Father:

- The Spirit "will teach you all things" (John 14:26).
- The Spirit "will remind you of everything I said to you" (John 14:26).
- The Spirit "will testify about me" (John 15:26).
- The Spirit "will guide you into all the truth" (John 16:13).
- The Spirit "will tell you what is yet to come" (John 16:13).

Today, the Spirit fulfills these same functions for us just as He did in the first century. And that's wonderful news!

Notes

Chapter 1: The Unexpected Voice of Jesus

1. Dante, *Inferno*, 1st canto, trans. Laurence Binyon.
2. Old German saying with literal translation as found in "European Sayings & Ideomatic Expressions," online database, accessed June 23, 2005, http://sayings.jacomac.de/details.php?id=43.
3. Mark 1:35; Matthew 14:23; Luke 4:42; Mark 6:46–48; Psalm 5:3, among others.
4. Hebrews 13:2.
5. John Wesley's commentary on Acts 16:7 in *Wesley's Notes on the Bible*, Christian Classics Ethereal Library, accessed December 7, 2015, http://www.ccel.org/ccel/wesley/notes.i.vi.xvii.html.
6. Pope John Paul II, quoted in Archbishop George Stack, *Unless the Tongue Catch Fire* (Leominster, UK: Gracewing, 2015), 15.
7. Author's paraphrase.
8. See, for example, Treadwell Walden's 1881 study *The Great Meaning of Metanoia* (Whitefish, MT: Kessinger, 2009), which asserts that *metanoia* conveys the essence of the Christian gospel. Therefore, Walden holds that no word in the New Testament can be greater than *metanoia*.
9. See commentary on Matthew 3:2 in A. T. Robertson, *Word Pictures in the New Testament* (Nashville: Broadman, 1933); *Encyclopedia of Religion and Ethics*, vol. 10, ed. James Hastings (New York: Scribner, 1919), sv. "Repentance."
10. Author's paraphrase (Matt. 3:11 and Luke 3:16).

Chapter 2: The Hidden Voice of Jesus

1. See John 19:25 and Luke 24:18. N. T. Wright is one among many scholars who believes that Cleopas and Clopas are the same individual. If true, his wife is named Mary.

2. Scholars disagree on how John 19:25 should be translated, but one likely translation is that Mary, wife of Clopas, was the sister of Jesus' mother. Interestingly, the second-century Christian chronicler Hegesippus wrote that Clopas was Joseph's brother. In this book, we are making Cleopas and Mary uncle and aunt to Jesus.

3. Note Isaiah 51:1 KJV: "Hearken to me, ye that follow after righteousness, ye that seek the LORD: look unto the rock whence ye are hewn, and to the hole of the pit whence ye are digged."

4. Conrad Gempf, *Jesus Asked* (Grand Rapids: Zondervan, 2003).

5. David Dark, *The Sacredness of Questioning Everything* (Grand Rapids: Zondervan, 2009).

6. Philip Kolb, ed., *Correspondence de Marcel Proust* (1930), vol. 19, quoted by Francis Steegmuller in *Times Literary Supplement* 22 (November 1991): 32.

7. Some have argued that the physical death of Christ resulted from rupture of the heart, and that the cavities of the heart and the surrounding vessels contained a watery fluid. See the various commentaries on John 19:34 available at http://biblehub.com/commentaries/john/19-34.htm.

8. The word *sincere* in Latin means "pure, whole, authentic, or without deceit" and can mean also "without wax," which referred to a piece of pottery that was in its natural state and not waxed over. If a piece of pottery broke in ancient times, one would mend the pieces together, and often the potter would use wax to fill in the cracks, then paint over it, hiding its defects. If you held it up to the light, however, you would quickly see the flaws. To buy a piece of pottery without wax (sincere) meant that the pot was unadulterated and authentic. God the Potter (an image that comes to us from Genesis) molds each of us and encourages us not to hide but to bear our scars proudly. To be a sincere bearer of the cross, you are not just honest, but broken and healed.

9. Augustine, as quoted in St. Thomas Aquinas's *Summa Theologica* (1273), trans. Fathers of the English Dominican Province (1912) (Raleigh: Hayes Barton Press, 2006), question 161, article 2.

10. Augustine, *Tractate* 9, on 1 John 4:17–21, n. 10 in *Tractates on the Gospel of John* 112–24; *Tractates on the First Epistle of John*, trans. John W. Rettig (Cincinnati: Catholic University of America Press, 1995), 259.

11. Saint Anthony, quoted in "Office of Readings—Memorial for Thursday in the 2nd Week of Lent," *The Liturgy of the Hours* (1974), http://divineoffice.org/0613-or/.

12. William Blake, in Theodore Roszak, *Where The Wasteland Ends: Politics and Transcendence in Postindustrial Society*, chap. 9, as cited at MindFire, accessed April 4, 2016, http://mindfire.ca/Mind%20on%20Fire%20-%20Blake%20-%20The%20Fourfold%20Vision.htm.

Chapter 3: The Elusive Voice of Jesus

1. John 10:7 KJV; John 10:9; Ephesians 2:20; John 2:19.

2. The Luke story of Jesus' third appearance happened directly after the Road to Emmaus. In fact, the Emmaus disciples were there in the room when Jesus appeared to all. The story in John happened on the evening of the day when Mary discovered Jesus was gone from the tomb. These could easily be the same story. We can't be sure, but the two gospel writers are most likely referring to the same appearance. Both scriptures begin with Jesus' shalom. John says Jesus breathed on them, showing His hands and side. Likewise, in Luke, Jesus showed His hands and side and invited them to see and touch. In a continuance from the Emmaus story, Jesus then opened their minds to the Scriptures, ate fish (so that they would believe He wasn't a ghost), and told them to stay in Jerusalem until He was clothed with power. John noted that when Jesus met His disciples by the sea, it was the third time He appeared to them all, which would make it even more likely that the Upper Room stories in Luke and John are referencing the same appearance. We call this the third appearance (after Mary and Emmaus), but it was the first to the disciples as a group. The Emmaus story involved only two disciples, not the Eleven of the inner circle. His next appearance would be the Thomas story, the next after that by the sea.

3. D. T. Niles, quoted in the *New York Times,* May 11, 1986, and reprinted in James B. Simpson's *Simpson's Contemporary Quotations* (Boston: Houghton Mifflin, 1988).

4. The phrase in Genesis 2:7 is *nishmat chayyim* (meaning and later indicated as *nishmat ruach chayyim*). See Genesis 7:21–22; 2 Samuel 22:16; Psalm 18:15–16. The verb means "to breathe with the spirit of God in order to create an animated, breathing, being." The definition denotes a spiritual element.

5. Gabriel Josipovici, *The Book of God* (New Haven: Yale University Press, 1988), 74.

6. Gene Greitenbach, in Leonard Sweet, *Post-Modern Pilgrims* (Nashville: B&H, 2000), 4.

Chapter 4: The Challenging Voice of Jesus

1. From Miles Smith's preface to the King James Version of the Bible (1611). See Barton Swaim, "God's English: The Making and Endurance of the King James Bible, 1611–2011," *Touchstone*, May/June 2011, http://www.touchstonemag.com/archives/article.php?id=24-03-023-f.
2. No text mentions the touching, according to Glenn W. Most in his book *Doubting Thomas:* "In over a thousand years of detailed, intense, devout exegesis of John 20, only two interpreters seemed to have recognized . . . that Thomas might not have actually touched Jesus: one Latin scholar, Augustine . . . and one Greek one, Zigabenus." (Cambridge, MA: Harvard University Press, 2005), 141.
3. Franz Kafka, quoted in Klaus Wagenbach, *Kafka* (Cambridge, MA: Harvard University Press, 2003), 52.
4. Alfred, Lord Tennyson, "In Memorium," in *The World's Best Poetry,* ed. Bliss Carman, et al. (Philadelphia: John D. Morris, 1904; Bartleby.com, 2012), http://www.bartleby.com/360/4/89.html.

Chapter 5: The Forgiving Voice of Jesus

1. This is the third time Jesus appeared to His disciples, and the fifth post-resurrection appearance. He previously appeared to Mary, but she wasn't technically one of the twelve disciples. For previous appearances see John 20:19–23, 26–29.
2. John H. Sammis, "Trust and Obey" (1887), v. 4, Hymnary.org, http://www.hymnary.org/media/fetch/138917.
3. "152-Year-Old Shipwreck Discovered in Great Lakes," *Maritime Executive*, December 9, 2013, http://www.maritime-executive.com/article/152Year Old-Shipwreck-Discovered-in-Great-Lakes-2013–12–09.
4. This insight comes from Dominican friar Timothy Radcliffe, former Master of the Order of Preachers, in his book *Why Go to Church?* (New York: Continuum, 2008), 19.
5. Quoted in Carl Arico, *A Taste of Silence* (New York: Continuum, 2007), 50.
6. Gregory of Nyssa, "Homily 5," *Homilies on the Song of Songs*, trans. Richard A. Norris Jr. (Atlanta: Society of Biblical Literature, 2012), 173.

Chapter 6: The Blinding Voice of Jesus

1. There are only two name changes in New Testament: from Simon to Peter and from Saul to Paul.
2. Augustine, Sermon 38.5, in *Nicene and Post-Nicene Fathers* 1, vol. 6, ed. Philip Schaff (Buffalo: Christian Literature Publishing, 1888); rev. and ed. for the New Advent website by Kevin Knight, http://www.newadvent.org/fathers/160338.htm.
3. William Hutchings, *Samuel Beckett's* Waiting for Godot: *A Reference Guide* (Westport, CT: Praeger, 2005), 48.
4. Oliver Wendell Holmes, "The Professor at the Breakfast Table," *Atlantic Monthly* 3 (January 1859): 85.
5. Emil Fackenheim, as quoted by Rabbi Amy R. Scheinerman, "Miracle: How We See and What We See," Judaism: Rabbi Scheinerman's Web Page, January 1999, http://www.scheinerman.net/judaism/Sermons/index.html.
6. Jenny Offill, *Dept. of Speculation* (n.p.: Granta, 2014), as quoted in *TLS*, June 27, 2014, 20.
7. William H. How, "For All the Saints Who from Their Labors Rest," 1864.
8. Jaroslav Pelikan, *The Vindication of Tradition* (New Haven: Yale University Press, 1984), 17.
9. Nicholas Buxton, *The Wilderness Within: Meditation and Modern Life* (Norwich, UK: Canterbury Press, 2014), 95–96.
10. C. S. Lewis, *The Problem of Pain* (San Francisco: HarperSanFrancisco, 1940, repr., 2001), 91.

Chapter 7: The Missional Voice of Jesus

1. William Blake, "Great things are done when Men & Mountains meet," from "Satiric Verses and Epigrams," in *The Complete Poetry and Prose of William Blake*, David V. Erdman, ed. (New York: Anchor, 1988), 511.
2. Exodus Rabbah 24:1.
3. These lines are found in the liturgies for many Catholic and Protestant services.
4. Martin Luther, *The Misuse of the Mass* (1522), quoted in Colin Morris, *The Sepulchre of Christ and the Medieval West* (New York: Oxford University Press, 2007), 365.
5. Abraham Joshua Heschel, *God in Search of Man* (New York: Farrar, Straus and Giroux, 1983), 98.
6. Here is the full quote from John Calvin's commentary on Psalm 127:2:

"The faithful, on the other hand, although they lead a laborious life, yet follow their vocations with composed and tranquil minds. Thus their hands are not idle, but their minds repose in the stillness of faith." John Calvin, *Commentary on Psalms*, Christian Classics Ethereal Library, http://www.ccel.org/ccel/calvin/calcom12.xi.i.html.

7. Genesis 1:26: "Let us make mankind in our image."

Chapter 8: The Godstruck Voice of Jesus

1. William Booth, *Salvation Army Songs* (New York: Savation Army Book Dept., 1911), 270.
2. Author's interpretation.
3. We keep pentecost in the Jewish tradition the way we keep *Shavuot* or keep the Passover. We celebrate it and remember it, we become part of it, and as we retell the story, it becomes our story too.
4. Science is not the enemy of faith. Science deals with facts; religion deals with truth.
5. Maximus the Confessor, *Ambiggum* 7, 1084 C-D.
6. Quoted in Richard Leonard, SJ, *Why Bother Praying* (New York: Paulist Press, 2013), chap. 5.
7. Christine Fleming Heffner, "The Parish Bake Shop," in *Parables for the Present* (Portland, OR: Hawthorne Books, 1974), 59.
8. Sir Laurens van der Post, *Jung and the Story of Our Time* (London: Hogarth Press, 1976), 39.
9. *Bruce Almighty*, directed by Tom Shadyac (Universal City, CA: Universal Pictures, 2003), motion picture.
10. Maltbie D. Babcock, "This Is My Father's World" (1901).

Chapter 11: Always Remain a Child

1. For a discussion on being childlike, see Leonard Sweet, *The Well-Played Life: Why Pleasing God Doesn't Have to Be Such Hard Work* (Carol Stream, IL: Tyndale, 2014).

Chapter 12: Exercise Faith

1. Anselm of Canterbury, *Proslogion*, in *Proslogian, with the Replies of Guanilo and Anselm*, trans. Thomas Williams (Indianapolis: Hackett, 1995), 6. Williams noted that Anselm was quoting Augustine, who himself was referencing an "older translation of Isaiah 7:9."

Notes

Chapter 13: Increasing Your Faith to Hear

1. George Campbell Morgan, *How to Live: The True Essentials of Life* (London: Parry Jackman, 1958), 77.

Chapter 17: The Lord's Voice in Scripture

1. "Break Thou the Bread of Life," 1877, words by Mary A. Lathbury, music by William Fiske Sherwin.

Chapter 19: What Does It Look Like?

1. Elizabeth Barrett Browning, "Aurora Leigh," in *Aurora Leigh and Other Poems* (New York: James Miller, 1872), 138.

Chapter 22: Visions and Dreams

1. Dallas Willard, *Hearing God* (Downers Grove, IL: IVP, 1999), 110–11.

Chapter 24: The Conscience

1. For a thorough discussion on the role of the human conscience in spiritual growth, see chapter 4 of *Jesus Now* by Frank Viola (Colorado Springs: David C. Cook, 2014).

Chapter 26: Four Ways to Recognize the Lord's Voice

1. Some who have been raised in legalistic traditions and may be given to abusing themselves may read into this ideas that we don't endorse. Self-denial and self-sacrifice do not mean self-loathing or self-scathing. Biblical self-denial springs from a healthy sense of our identity in Jesus Christ as beloved children of God. When we're following the Spirit of Jesus, we put others ahead of ourselves, laying down our lives. Love is seeking the benefit of others at the expense of our own selfish desires.

Chapter 29: Hearing the Voice in the Morning

1. Charles H. Spurgeon, *Lectures to My Students* (London: Passmore and Alabaster, 1877).

Chapter 30: Hearing the Voice While Walking

1. A. B. Simpson, "O Lord, Breathe Thy Spirit on Me."

Chapter 31: Hearing the Voice in Worship

1. Leonard Sweet and Frank Viola, *Jesus Manifesto: Restoring the Supremacy and Sovereignty of Jesus Christ* (Nashville: Thomas Nelson, 2010), xv.

Chapter 32: Personalizing the Voice in Scripture

1. Leonard Sweet and Frank Viola, *Jesus Manifesto* (Nashville: Thomas Nelson, 2010), 176–77.

Chapter 35: The Challenge of Our Expectations

1. See my book, *God's Favorite Place on Earth,* where I discuss this problem and offer solutions.

Chapter 37: The Danger of Counterfeit Voices

1. See, for example, Martin Luther in *Table Talk*: "For, where God build a church there the devil would also build a chapel." Martin Luther, *Table Talk*, trans. William Hazlitt, repr. (Grand Rapids, MI: Christian Classics Ethereal Library), http://www.ccel.org/ccel/luther/tabletalk.pdf, lxvii.
2. See *War on the Saints* by Jesse Penn-Lewis (Fort Washington, PA: CLC Ministries, 2004, originally published in 1964) for details.
3. Frank Viola, "Jesus and Paul Under Fire," *Beyond Evangelical: The Blog of Frank Viola*, October 1, 2012, http://frankviola.org/jesusandpaul.
4. I share more about spiritual counterfeits, as well as the baptism of the Holy Spirit and spiritual gifts, in my book *Rethinking the Spirit*, which is part of my Rethinking Series, available at RethinkingSeries.com.

Chapter 39: The Danger of Misunderstanding

1. See *Revise Us Again* for a discussion on the threefold way in which God communicates to His children (chapter 1) and the three spiritual conversational styles that Christians employ without even realizing it (chapter 4).

Chapter 40: The Danger of Misrepresenting God

1. Frank Viola, *Revise Us Again: Living from a Renewed Christian Script* (Colorado Springs: David C. Cook, 2010), chap. 2.
2. Oswald Chambers, "The Distraction of Contempt," in *My Utmost for His Highest*, online at http://utmost.org/the-distraction-of-contempt/.

Chapter 42: The Danger of Misinterpreting Dry Spells and Dark Nights

1. See Frank Viola, *Revise Us Again: Living from a Renewed Christian Script* (Colorado Springs: David C. Cook, 2010), chap. 6.

Chapter 43: The Goal of It All

1. William Temple, "The Divinity of Christ," in B. H. Streeter et al., *Foundations: A Statement of Christian Belief in Terms of Modern Thought*, (London: MacMillian, 1912), 259.
2. For details on God's eternal purpose, see Frank Viola, *From Eternity to Here: Rediscovering the Ageless Purpose of God* (Colorado Springs, CO: David C. Cook, 2009).

About the Authors

Leonard **Sweet** is author of more than sixty-five books and thousands of published sermons. He is the owner and primary writer for preachthestory.com, a growing, innovative resource for preachers. Dr. Sweet is the E. Stanley Jones Chair of Evangelism at Drew University and distinguished visiting professor at both George Fox Evangelical Seminary and Tabor College. He is a world-renowned speaker and preacher and has been voted one of the most influential Christians in America. His Napkin Scribbles podcasts, as well as sermons, videos, and blog posts are available at preachthestory.com, and his books and resources are listed on leonardsweet.com.

Frank **Viola** has helped thousands of people around the world to deepen their relationship with Jesus Christ and enter into a more vibrant and authentic experience of church. His mission is to help serious followers of Jesus know their Lord more deeply so they can experience real transformation and make a lasting impact. Viola has written many books on these themes, including *God's Favorite Place on Earth*, *From Eternity to Here*, and *Jesus Manifesto* (with Leonard Sweet). His blog, frankviola.org, is rated as one of the most popular in Christian circles today.

Want to Delve Deeper?

Check out Frank Viola's discipleship course, *Learning How to Live by the Indwelling Life of Christ*. A ten-part audio program with workbook and action plans.

For details, go to TheDeeperJourney.com.

For more on how to help others live the ongoing life of Christ, see preachthestory.com.

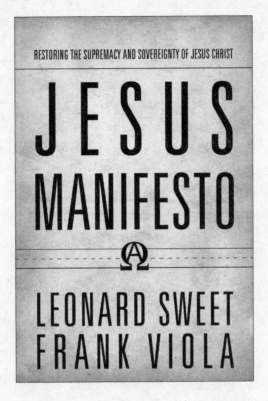

RESTORING THE SUPREMACY AND SOVEREIGNTY OF JESUS CHRIST

JESUS MANIFESTO

LEONARD SWEET FRANK VIOLA

"So that in everything He might have the supremacy."
—Colossians 1:18

Jesus Manifesto presents a fresh unveiling of Jesus as not only Savior and Lord, but as so much more. It is a prophetic call to restore the supremacy and sovereignty of Christ in a world—and a church—that has lost sight of Him.

Read this book and see your Lord like you've never seen Him before.

AVAILABLE WHEREVER BOOKS AND EBOOKS ARE SOLD.